RĀJA-VIDYĀ

The KING OF KNOWLEDGE

ALL GLORY TO ŚRĪ GURU AND GAURĀṄGA

RĀJA-VIDYĀ

The KING OF KNOWLEDGE

His Divine Grace
A.C. Bhaktivedanta Swami Prabhupāda

Founder-Ācārya
International Society for Krishna Consciousness

THE BHAKTIVEDANTA BOOK TRUST
New York · Los Angeles · London · Bombay

Readers interested in the subject matter
of this book are invited by
the International Society for Krishna Consciousness
to correspond with its Secretary.

International Society for Krishna Consciousness
3959 Landmark Street
Culver City, California 90230

First Printing, 1973:
100,000 copies

Library of Congress Catalog Card Number: 72-84845
International Standard Book Number: 0-912776-40-4

Printed in the United States of America by ISKCON Press

contents

1

Rāja-Vidyā: The King of Knowledge

śrī bhagavān uvāca
idaṁ tu te guhyatamaṁ
pravakṣyāmy anasūyave
jñānaṁ vijñāna-sahitaṁ
yaj jñātvā mokṣyase 'śubhāt

"The Supreme Lord said: My dear Arjuna, because you are never envious of Me, I shall impart to you this most secret wisdom, knowing which you shall be relieved of the miseries of material existence." (Bg. 9.1)

The opening words of the Ninth Chapter of *Bhagavad-gītā* indicate that the Supreme Godhead is speaking. Here Śrī Kṛṣṇa is referred to as Bhagavān. *Bhaga* means opulences, and *vān* means one who possesses. We have some conception of God, but in the Vedic literature there are definite descriptions and definitions of what is meant by God, and what is meant is described in one word—Bhagavān. Bhagavān possesses all opulences, the totality of knowledge, wealth, power, beauty, fame and renunciation. When we find someone who possesses these opulences in full, we are to know that he is God. There are many rich, wise, famous, beautiful and powerful men, but no one man can claim to possess all of these opulences. Only Kṛṣṇa claims to possess them in totality.

bhoktāraṁ yajña-tapasāṁ
sarva-loka-maheśvaram
suhṛdaṁ sarva-bhūtānāṁ
jñātvā māṁ śāntim ṛcchati

"The sages, knowing Me as the ultimate purpose of all sacrifices and austerities, the Supreme Lord of all planets and demigods and the benefactor and well-wisher of all living entities, attain peace from the pangs of material miseries." (Bg. 5.29)

Here Kṛṣṇa proclaims that He is the enjoyer of all activities and the proprietor of all planets *(sarva-loka-maheśvaram).* An individual may possess a large tract of land, and he may be proud of his ownership, but Kṛṣṇa claims to possess all planetary systems. Kṛṣṇa also claims to be the friend of all living entities *(suhṛdaṁ sarva-bhūtānām).* When a person understands that God is the proprietor of everything, the friend of everyone and the enjoyer of all, he becomes very peaceful. This is the actual peace formula. No one can have peace as long as he thinks, "I am the proprietor." Who is capable of claiming proprietorship? Only a few hundred years ago the red Indians were considered to be the proprietors of America. Today we in our turn are claiming that proprietorship, but in four hundred or a thousand years perhaps someone else will come to claim the same. The land is here, and we come here and falsely claim ourselves to be proprietors of it. This philosophy of false proprietorship is not in line with Vedic injunctions. *Śrī Īśopaniṣad* states that "everything animate or inanimate that is within the universe is controlled and owned by the Lord *(īśāvāsyam idaṁ sarvam).*" The truth of this statement is factual, but under illusion we are thinking that we are the proprietors. In actuality God owns everything, and therefore He is called the richest.

Of course there are many men who claim to be God. In India, for instance, at any time, one has no difficulty in finding at least one dozen people claiming to be God. But if you ask them if they are the proprietor of everything, they find this difficult to answer. This is a criterion by which we can understand who God is. God is the proprietor of everything, and, being so, He must be more powerful than anyone or anything else. When Kṛṣṇa was personally present on this earth, no one could conquer Him. There is no record of His ever having lost a battle. He belonged to a *kṣatriya* (warrior) family, and the *kṣatriyas* are meant to give protection to the weak. As far as His opulence is concerned, He married 16,108 wives. Every wife had her own separate palace, and Kṛṣṇa expanded Himself 16,108 times in order to enjoy them all. This may seem difficult to believe, but it is stated in *Śrīmad-Bhāgavatam,* and the great sages of India recognize this as scripture and recognize Kṛṣṇa as God.

In the first verse of this Ninth Chapter, by the word *guhyatamam,* Śrī Kṛṣṇa intimates that He is imparting the most confidential knowledge to Arjuna. Why is He proclaiming this to Arjuna? It is because Arjuna is *anasūyu*—non-envious. In the material world if someone is greater than us, we are envious. We are not only envious of one another, but of God. Also when Kṛṣṇa says, "I am the proprietor," we disbelieve it. But this is not the case with Arjuna, who listens to Kṛṣṇa without envy. Arjuna does not cavil with Kṛṣṇa but agrees with whatever He says. This is his special qualification, and this is the way of understanding *Bhagavad-gītā.* It is not possible to understand what God is by our own mental speculations; we have to hear, and we have to accept.

Because Arjuna is not envious, Kṛṣṇa speaks this special knowledge to him. This is not only theoretical knowledge but practical knowledge *(vijñāna-sahitam).* Whatever knowledge we receive from *Bhagavad-gītā* should not be taken for sentimentality or fanaticism. The knowledge is both *jñāna* and *vijñāna,* theoretical wisdom and scientific knowledge. If one becomes well-versed in this knowledge, liberation is certain. Life in this material world is by nature inauspicious and miserable. *Mokṣa* means liberation, and the promise is that by dint of understanding this knowledge one will attain liberation from all miseries. It is important then to understand what Kṛṣṇa says about this knowledge.

rāja-vidyā rāja-guhyaṁ
pavitram idam uttamam
pratyakṣāvagamaṁ dharmyaṁ
susukhaṁ kartum avyayam

"This knowledge is the king of education, the most secret of all secrets. It is the purest knowledge, and because it gives direct perception of the self by realization, it is the perfection of religion. It is everlasting, and it is joyfully performed." (Bg. 9.2)

According to *Bhagavad-gītā,* the topmost knowledge *(rāja-vidyā rāja-guhyam)* is Kṛṣṇa consciousness because in *Bhagavad-gītā* we find that the symptom of one who is actually in knowledge is that he has surrendered unto Kṛṣṇa. As long as we go on speculating about God but do not surrender, it is understood that we have not attained the perfection of knowledge. The perfection of knowledge is:

bahūnāṁ janmanām ante
jñānavān māṁ prapadyate
vāsudevaḥ sarvam iti
sa mahātmā sudurlabhaḥ

"After many births and deaths, he who is actually in knowledge surrenders unto Me, knowing Me to be the cause of all causes and all that is. Such a great soul is very rare." (Bg. 7.19)

As long as we do not surrender, we cannot understand God. Surrender to God may take many births, but if we accept that God is great, it is possible to surrender unto Him immediately. But generally this is not our position in the material world. We are characteristically envious and consequently think, "Oh, why should I surrender unto God? I am independent. I shall work independently." Therefore in order to rectify this misgiving, we have to work for many births. In this regard, the name of Kṛṣṇa is especially significant. *Kṛṣ* means "repetition of birth," and *na* means "one who checks." Our repetition of birth can be checked only by God. No one can check his repetition of birth and death without the causeless mercy of God.

The subject matter of the Ninth Chapter is *rāja-vidyā. Rāja* means "king," and *vidyā* means "knowledge." In ordinary life we find one person king in one subject and another in another subject. This knowledge, however, is sovereign over all others, and all other knowledge is subject or relative to it. The word *rāja-guhyam* indicates that this sovereign knowledge is very confidential, and the word *pavitram* means that it is very pure. This knowledge is also *uttamam; ud* means "transcend," and *tama* means "darkness," and that knowledge which surpasses this world and the knowledge of this world is called *uttamam.* It is the knowledge of light, and darkness has been separated from it. If one follows this path of knowledge, he will personally understand how far he has progressed down the path of perfection *(pratyakṣāvagamaṁ dharmyam). Susukhaṁ kartum* indicates that this knowledge is very happy and joyful to execute. And *avyayam* indicates that this knowledge is permanent. We may work in this material world for education or riches, but these things are not *avyayam,* for as soon as this body is finished, everything else is also finished. With death, our education, advanced degrees, bank balances, family—everything—are all finished. Whatever we're doing in this material world is not eternal. However, this knowledge is not like that.

nehābhikrama-nāśo 'sti
pratyavāyo na vidyate
svalpam apy asya dharmasya
trāyate mahato bhayāt

"In this endeavor there is no loss or diminution, and a little advancement on this path can protect one from the most dangerous type of fear." (Bg. 2.40)

Knowledge in Kṛṣṇa consciousness is so perfect that if one performs work in Kṛṣṇa consciousness and yet does not attain perfection, in his next life he takes up from wherever he left off. In other words, actions performed in Kṛṣṇa consciousness are durable. On the other hand, material achievements, because they pertain to the body, are vanquished at death. Knowledge that pertains to designations does not endure. I am thinking that I am a man or a woman, an American or Indian, a Christian or Hindu—these are all designations pertaining to the body, and when the body is finished, they will also be finished. We are actually spirit, and therefore our spiritual activities will go with us wherever we go.

Śrī Kṛṣṇa indicates that this king of knowledge is also happily performed. We can easily see that activities in Kṛṣṇa consciousness are joyfully done. There is chanting and dancing, eating *prasādam* (food that has been offered to Kṛṣṇa) and discussing *Bhagavad-gītā.* These are the main processes. There are no stringent rules and regulations that we have to sit so straight for so long or do so many gymnastics, or control our breath. No, the process is very easily and happily done. Everyone wants to dance, to sing, to eat and to hear the truth. This process is truly *susukham*—very happy.

In the material world there are so many gradations of education. Some people never finish grammar school or high school, whereas others go on and receive a university education, a BA, MA, PhD, and so on. But what is this *rāja-vidyā,* the king of education, the *summum bonum* of knowledge? It is this

Kṛṣṇa consciousness. Real knowledge is understanding "what I am." Unless we come to the point of understanding what we are, we cannot attain real knowledge. When Sanātana Gosvāmī left his government post and came to Caitanya Mahāprabhu for the first time, he asked the Lord, "What is education?" Although Sanātana Gosvāmī knew a number of languages, including Sanskrit, he still inquired about real education. "The general populace calls me highly educated," Sanātana Gosvāmī told the Lord, "and I am such a fool that I actually believe them."

The Lord replied, "Why should you not think you're well educated? You're a great scholar in Sanskrit and Persian."

"That may be," Sanātana Gosvāmī said, "but I do not know what I am." He then went on to tell the Lord: "I do not wish to suffer, but these material miseries are forced upon me. I neither know where I've come from nor where I'm going, but people are calling me educated. When they call me a great scholar, I am satisfied, but in truth I am such a great fool that I know not what I am." Sanātana Gosvāmī was actually speaking for all of us, for this is our present situation. We may be proud of our academic education, but if asked what we are, we are not able to say. Everyone is under the conception that this body is the self, but we learn from Vedic sources that this is not so. Only after realizing that we are not these bodies can we enter into real knowledge and understand what we actually are. This then, is the beginning of knowledge.

Rāja-vidyā may be further defined as not only knowing what one is, but acting accordingly. If we do not know who we are, how can our activities be proper? If we are mistaken about our identity, we will also be mistaken about our activities. Simply knowing that we are not these material bodies is not sufficient; we must act according to the conviction that we are spiritual. Action based on this knowledge—spiritual activity—is work in Kṛṣṇa consciousness. This kind of knowledge may not seem to be so easily attainable, but it is made very easy by the mercy of Kṛṣṇa and Lord Caitanya Mahāprabhu who made this knowledge easily available through the process of chanting Hare Kṛṣṇa, Hare Kṛṣṇa, Kṛṣṇa Kṛṣṇa, Hare Hare/ Hare Rāma, Hare Rāma, Rāma Rāma, Hare Hare.

Caitanya Mahāprabhu divided the living entities into two major categories: those that are moving and those that are not moving. Trees, grass, plants, stones, etc., do not move because they do not have sufficiently developed consciousness. Their consciousness is there, but is covered. If a living being does not understand his position, he is stonelike, although dwelling in a human body. The living entities—birds, reptiles, animals, insects, human beings, demigods, etc.—number over 8,000,000 species, and of these a very small number are human beings. Lord Caitanya further points out that out of 400,000 species of human beings, some are civilized; and out of many civilized persons, there are only a few who are devoted to the scriptures.

In the present day most people claim to be devoted to some religion—Christian, Hindu, Moslem, Buddhist, etc.—but in fact they do not really believe in the scriptures. Those who do believe in the scriptures are, by and large, attached to pious philanthropic activities. They believe that religion means *yajña* (sacrifice), *dāna* (charity) and *tapas* (penance). One who engages in *tapasya* undertakes voluntarily very rigid regulations, such as *brahmacārī* students (celibates) or *sannyāsīs* (renounced order) undertake. Charity means voluntarily giving away one's material possessions. In the present age there is no sacrifice, but from historical literatures like the *Mahābhārata* we get information that kings performed sacrifices by distributing rubies, gold and silver. *Yajña* was primarily for kings, and charity, on a much smaller scale, was meant for householders. Those who actually believed in scriptures usually adopted some of these principles. But generally in this age people simply say that they belong to a religion but in actuality do nothing. Out of millions of such people, a very small number actually perform charity, sacrifice and penance. Caitanya Mahāprabhu further points out that out of millions who perform such religious principles all over the universe, only a few attain perfect knowledge and understand what they are .

Just knowing "I am not this body but am spirit soul" is not sufficient. We have to escape this entanglement of material nature. This is called *mukti*, liberation. Out of many thousands of persons who are in self-knowledge as to what and who they are, only one or two may be actually liberated. And out of many thousands who are liberated, only one or two may understand what and who Kṛṣṇa is. So understanding Kṛṣṇa is not such an easy job. Thus in this age of Kali, an age characterized by ignorance and chaos, liberation is out of the reach of practically everyone. One has to go through the whole ordeal of becoming civilized, then religious, and then one has to perform charities and sacrifices and come to the platform of knowledge, then to the stage of liberation, and finally, after liberation, to the understanding of what Kṛṣṇa is. This process is also indicated in *Bhagavad-gītā:*

brahma-bhūtaḥ prasannātmā
na śocati na kāṅkṣati
samaḥ sarveṣu bhūteṣu
mad-bhaktiṁ labhate parām

"One who is thus transcendentally situated at once realizes the Supreme Brahman. He never laments or desires to have anything; he is equally disposed to every living entity. In that state he attains pure devotional service unto Me." (Bg. 18.54)

These are the signs of liberation. The first symptom of one who is liberated is that he is very happy. It is not possible to find him morose. Nor does he have any anxiety. He never frets, "This thing I don't have. Oh, I must secure this thing. Oh, this bill I have to pay. I have to go here, there." One who is liberated has no anxieties at all. He may be the poorest man in the world, but he neither laments nor thinks that he is poor. Why should he think that he is poor? When we think that we are these material bodies and that we have possessions to go with them, then we think that we are poor or rich, but one who is liberated from the material conception of life has nothing to do with possessions or lack of possessions. "I have nothing to lose and nothing to gain," he thinks. "I am completely separate from all this." Nor does he see anyone else as rich or poor, educated or uneducated, beautiful or ugly, etc. He does not see any material dualities, for his vision is completely on the spiritual platform, and he sees that every living entity is part and parcel of Kṛṣṇa. Thus seeing all entities in their true identity, he tries to take them back to Kṛṣṇa consciousness. His viewpoint is that everyone—whether he be *brāhmaṇa* or *śūdra,* black or white, Hindu, Christian, or whatever—should come to Kṛṣṇa consciousness. When one is situated in this way, then: *mad-bhaktiṁ labhate parām*—he becomes eligible for becoming a pure devotee of Kṛṣṇa's.

Practically speaking, this process is not very easy in this age of Kali. In *Śrīmad-Bhāgavatam* a description is given of the people of this age. Their duration of life is said to be very short, they tend to be phlegmatic and slow and to sleep a great deal, and when they're not sleeping, they are busy earning money. At the most they only have two hours a day for spiritual activities, so what is the hope for spiritual understanding? It is also stated that even if one is anxious to make spiritual progress, there are many pseudo-spiritual societies to take advantage of him. People are also characterized in this age as being unfortunate. They have a great deal of difficulty meeting the primary demands of life—eating, defending, mating, and sleeping—necessities which are met even by the animals. Even if people are meeting these necessities in this age, they are always anxious about war, either defending themselves from aggressors or having to go to war themselves. In addition to this, there are always disturbing diseases and economic problems in Kali-yuga. Therefore Lord Śrī Kṛṣṇa considered that in this age it is impossible for people to come to the perfectional stage of liberation by following the prescribed rules and regulations.

Thus out of His causeless mercy, Śrī Kṛṣṇa came as Lord Caitanya Mahāprabhu and distributed the means to the highest perfection of life and spiritual ecstasy by the chanting of Hare Kṛṣṇa, Hare Kṛṣṇa, Kṛṣṇa Kṛṣṇa, Hare Hare/ Hare Rāma, Hare Rāma, Rāma Rāma, Hare Hare. This process of chanting is most practical, and it does not depend on whether one is liberated or not, or whether one's condition is conducive to spiritual life or not—whoever takes to this process becomes immediately purified. Therefore it is called *pavitram* (pure). Furthermore, for one who takes to this Kṛṣṇa consciousness process, the seeds of latent reactions to his sinful actions are all nullified. Just as a fire turns whatever we put into it to ashes, this process turns to ashes all the sinful reactions of our past lives.

We must understand that our suffering is due to our sinful activity, and sinful activity is due to our ignorance. Sins, or transgressions, are committed by those who do not know what is what. A child, for instance, will naively put his hand in a fire because of ignorance. He is thus burned immediately, for the fire is impartial and does not allow any special consideration for the innocent child.

It will simply act as fire. Similarly, we do not know how this material world is functioning, who its controller is, nor how it is controlled, and due to our ignorance we act in foolish ways, but nature is so stringent that she does not allow us to escape the reactions to our actions. Whether we commit an act knowingly or unknowingly, the reactions and consequent sufferings are there. However, through knowledge we can understand what the actual situation is, who God is, and what our relationship with Him is.

This knowledge by which we can gain release from suffering is possible in the human form of life, not in the animal form. To give us knowledge, to give us proper direction, there are scriptures written in various languages in all parts of the world. Lord Caitanya Mahāprabhu pointed out that people are forgetful from time immemorial about their relationship with the Supreme Lord; therefore Kṛṣṇa has sent so many representatives to impart the scriptures to man. We should take advantage of these, especially of *Bhagavad-gītā,* which is the prime scripture for the modern world.

2
Knowledge Beyond Saṁsāra

Kṛṣṇa specifically states that this process of Kṛṣṇa consciousness is *susukham,* very pleasant and easy to practice. Indeed, the devotional process is very pleasant; we melodiously sing with instruments, and someone will listen and also join *(śravaṇaṁ kīrtanam).* Of course the music should be in relation with the Supreme Lord, in glorification of Him. Hearing *Bhagavad-gītā* is also part of devotional service, and in addition to hearing it one should be eager to apply it in his life. Kṛṣṇa consciousness is a science and should not be accepted blindly. There are nine processes of devotional service recommended (hearing, chanting, remembering, worshiping, praying, serving, engaging as a servitor of the Lord, establishing friendly relations with the Lord, offering everything to the Lord). These are all easy to practice and should be joyfully performed.

Of course if one thinks that *Bhagavad-gītā* and the Hare Kṛṣṇa *mantra* are part of the Hindu system and doesn't want to accept them because of this, he can nonetheless attend the Christian church and sing there. There is no difference between this process and that process; the point is whatever process one follows, he must become God conscious. God is neither Moslem nor Hindu nor Christian—He is God. Nor are we to be considered Hindu, Moslem or Christian. These are bodily designations. We are all pure spirit, part and parcel of the Supreme. God is *pavitram,* pure, and we are also pure. Somehow or other, however, we have fallen into this material ocean, and as the waves toss, we suffer. Actually we have nothing to do with the tossing waves of material miseries. We must simply pray, "Kṛṣṇa, please pick me up." As soon as we forget Kṛṣṇa, the ocean of illusion is there, and it at once captures us. The chanting of Hare Kṛṣṇa is most important in order to escape from this ocean. Hare Kṛṣṇa, Hare Kṛṣṇa, Kṛṣṇa Kṛṣṇa, Hare Hare/ Hare Rāma, Hare Rāma, Rāma Rāma, Hare Hare is a sound *(śabda)* that is non-different from Kṛṣṇa. The sound Kṛṣṇa and the original Kṛṣṇa are the same. When we chant Hare Kṛṣṇa and dance, Kṛṣṇa is also dancing with us. Of course we may say, "Well, I do not see Him," but why do we put so much stress on seeing? Why not hearing? Seeing, tasting, smelling, touching, and hearing are all instruments for experience and knowledge. Why do we put such exclusive stress on seeing? A devotee does not wish to see Kṛṣṇa; he is satisfied by simply hearing of Kṛṣṇa. Seeing may eventually be there, but hearing should not be considered any less important. There are things which we hear but do not see—the wind may be whistling past our ears, and we can hear it, but there is no possibility of seeing the wind. Since hearing is no less an important experience or valid one than seeing, we can hear Kṛṣṇa and realize His presence through sound. Śrī Kṛṣṇa Himself says, "I am not there in My abode, or in the heart of the meditating *yogī* but where my pure devotees are singing." We can feel the presence of Kṛṣṇa as we actually make progress.

It is not that we should simply take things from Kṛṣṇa and offer Him nothing. Everyone is taking something from God, so why not give something? We are taking from Kṛṣṇa so much light, air, food, water and so on. Unless these resources are supplied by Kṛṣṇa, no one can live. Is it love to simply keep taking and taking and taking without ever offering anything in return? Love means taking and giving also. If we just take from someone and give him nothing in return, that is not love–it is exploitation. It is not that we should just continue eating without ever offering anything to Kṛṣṇa. In *Bhagavad-gītā* Kṛṣṇa says:

patraṁ puṣpaṁ phalaṁ toyaṁ
yo me bhaktyā prayacchati
tad ahaṁ bhakty-upahṛtam
aśnāmi prayatātmanaḥ

yat karoṣi yad aśnāsi
yaj juhoṣi dadāsi yat
yat tapasyasi kaunteya
tat kuruṣva mad arpaṇam

"If one offers Me with love and devotion a leaf, a flower, fruit or water, I will accept it. O son of Kuntī, all that you do, all that you eat, all that you offer and give away, as well as all austerities that you perform, should be done as an offering unto Me." (Bg. 9.26-27)

In addition to giving and receiving, in the execution of devotional service one has to submit to

Kṛṣṇa whatever distress or confidential problem he has. He should say, "Kṛṣṇa, I am suffering in this way. I have fallen in this tossing ocean of material illusion. Kindly pick me up. I understand now that I have no identification with this material world. I am simply put here, as if thrown into the Atlantic ocean. I may not in any way identify with the Atlantic ocean, but I am subject to the tossing of the ocean. Actually I am a spiritual spark, a fragmental part of You." To our misfortune, we try to identify with this ocean and stop its tossing. We must not try to stop the tossing. It is not possible. In any case, the tossing will go on, for that is the law of nature. Only the foolish try to adjust to this world; the real problem is how to get out of it. Those who do attempt to adjust and who never turn to Kṛṣṇa are continually subject to transmigration in the ocean of birth and death.

aśraddadhānāḥ puruṣā
dharmasyāsya parantapa
aprāpya māṁ nivartante
mṛtyu-saṁsāra-vartmani

"Those who are not faithful on the path of devotional service cannot attain Me, O conqueror of foes, but return to birth and death in this material world." (Bg. 9.3)

By definition, religion is that which connects us with God. If it is not capable of connecting us with God, it is no religion. Religion means searching for God, understanding God and establishing a relationship with God. This is religion. Those who are engaged in devotional service are acting for Kṛṣṇa or God, and since in this way there is connection with God, Kṛṣṇa consciousness is a religion.

It is not possible to manufacture a religion. A true religion must come from an authorized source, and that source is either God or His representative. Religion has been called the law of God. It is not possible for a person to manufacture a State law. The law is there, and it is given by the State. One may create some bylaws for his own society, but these laws must be sanctioned by the law of the State. Similarly, if we wish to make some principle of religion, it must be sanctioned by the Vedic authority.

Bhagavad-gītā is also religion. Great authorities like Rāmānujācārya, Madhvācārya, Viṣṇusvāmī, Lord Caitanya, Śaṅkarācārya, and so many others have accepted *Bhagavad-gītā* as the supreme principle of religion and Kṛṣṇa as the Supreme Personality of Godhead. There is no doubt about it. In the West also *Bhagavad-gītā* is accepted as a great book of philosophy, and many great scholars and philosophers in the West have read it and commented upon it. Despite acceptance by the scholars and *ācāryas,* there are persons who do not accept *Bhagavad-gītā* and who have no faith. They do not accept it at all as authority, for they think that it is some sentimental exaggeration by a man known as Kṛṣṇa. Thus Kṛṣṇa states in the above quoted verse that those who reject *Bhagavad-gītā* as authority cannot have any connection with Him, and because they have no relation to Him, they remain in the cycle of birth and death. *Aprāpya māṁ nivartante mṛtyu-saṁsāra-vartmani.* Being subjected to *saṁsāra,* the cycle of birth and death, does not guarantee that one will necessarily get a similar facility for understanding *Bhagavad-gītā* in the next life. One may not necessarily be born again as a human being, or in America, or in India, or even on this planet. There is no certainty; it all depends on our work. On the path of birth and death we take our birth, remain for some time, enjoy or suffer, then again give up this body and enter into the womb of a mother, either human being or animal, then prepare another body to come out and begin our work again. This is called *mṛtyu-saṁsāra-vartmani.* If one wants to avoid this path, he must take to Kṛṣṇa consciousness.

When Yudhiṣṭhira Mahārāja was asked, "What is the most wonderful thing in the world?" he replied, "The most wonderful thing is that every day, every moment, people are dying, and yet everyone thinks that death will not come for him." Every minute and every second we experience that living entities are going to the temple of death. Men, insects, animals, birds—everyone is going. This world, therefore, is called *mṛtyuloka*—the planet of death. Every day there are obituaries, and if we bother to go to the cemetery or crematorium grounds we can validate them. Yet everyone is thinking, "Somehow or other I'll live." Everyone is subject to the law of death, yet no one takes it seriously. This is illusion. Thinking we will live forever, we go on doing whatever we like, feeling that we will never be held responsible. This is a very risky life, and it is the densest part of illusion. We should become very serious and understand that death is waiting. We have heard the expression, "as sure as death." This means that in this world death is the most certain thing; no one can avoid it. When death comes, no longer will our puffed-up philosophy or advanced degrees help us. At that time our stout and strong body and our intelligence—which don't care for anything—are vanquished. At that time the fragmental portion (*jīvātmā*) comes under the dictation of material nature, and *prakṛti* (nature) gives us the type of body for which we are fit. If we want to take this risk, we can avoid Kṛṣṇa; if we don't want to take it, Kṛṣṇa will come to help us.

3

Knowledge of Kṛṣṇa's Energies

It may be noted at this point that the Ninth Chapter of *Bhagavad-gītā* is especially meant for those who have already accepted Śrī Kṛṣṇa as the Supreme Personality of Godhead. In other words, it is meant for His devotees. If one does not accept Śrī Kṛṣṇa as the Supreme, this Ninth Chapter will appear as something different from what it actually is. As stated in the beginning, the subject matter of the Ninth Chapter is the most confidential material in the entire *Bhagavad-gītā*. If one doesn't accept Kṛṣṇa as the Supreme, he will think the chapter to be a mere exaggeration. This is especially the case with the verses dealing with Kṛṣṇa's relationship with His creation.

mayā tatam idaṁ sarvaṁ
jagad avyakta-mūrtinā
mat-sthāni sarva-bhūtāni
na cāhaṁ teṣv avasthitaḥ

"By Me, in My unmanifested form, this entire universe is pervaded. All beings are in Me, but I am not in them." (Bg. 9.4)

The world which we see is also Kṛṣṇa's energy, His *māyā*. Here, *mayā* means "by Me," as if one says, "This work has been done by me." This "by Me" does not mean that He has done His work and has finished or retired. If I start a large factory and I say,

"This factory was started by me," in no case should it be concluded that I am lost or in any way not present. Although a manufacturer may refer to his products as being "manufactured by me," it does not mean that he personally created or constructed his product, but that the product was produced by his energy. Similarly, if Kṛṣṇa says, "Whatever you see in the world was created by Me," we are not to suppose that He is no longer existing.

It is not very difficult to see God everywhere in the creation, for He is everywhere present. Just as in the Ford factory the workers see Mr. Ford in every corner, those who are conversant with the science of Kṛṣṇa can see Him in every atom of the creation. Everything is resting on Kṛṣṇa (*mat-sthāni sarva bhūtāni*), but Kṛṣṇa is not there (*na cāhaṁ teṣv avasthitaḥ). Kṛṣṇa and His energy are non-different, yet the energy is not Kṛṣṇa. The sun and the sunshine are not different, but the sunshine is not the sun. The sunshine may come through our window and enter our room, but this is not to say that the sun is in our room. The *Viṣṇu Purāṇa* states: *parasya brahmaṇaḥ śaktiḥ: parasya* means supreme, *brahmaṇaḥ* means Absolute Truth, and *śaktiḥ* means energy. The energy of the Supreme Absolute is everything, but in that energy Kṛṣṇa is not to be found.

There are two kinds of energy—material and spiritual. *Jīvas,* or individual souls, belong to the superior energy of Kṛṣṇa, but because they are prone to be attracted to the material energy, they are called marginal energy. But actually there are only two energies. All of the planetary systems and universes are resting on the energies of Kṛṣṇa. Just as all the planets in the solar system are resting in the sunshine, everything within the creation is resting on Kṛṣṇa-shine. All of these potencies of the Lord give pleasure to a devotee, but one who is envious of Kṛṣṇa rejects them. When one is a nondevotee, the statements of Kṛṣṇa seem to be so much bluff, but when one is a devotee, he thinks, "Oh, my Lord is so powerful," and he becomes filled with love and adoration. Nondevotees think that because Kṛṣṇa says, "I am God," they and everyone else can say the same. But if asked to show their universal form, they cannot do it. That is the difference between a pseudo god and the real God. Kṛṣṇa's pastimes cannot be imitated. Kṛṣṇa married over 16,000 wives and kept them nicely in 16,000 palaces, but an ordinary man cannot even keep one wife nicely. It is not that Kṛṣṇa just spoke so many wonderful things; He also acted wonderfully. We should not believe one thing that Kṛṣṇa says or does and reject another; if belief is there, it must be full belief.

In this regard, there is a story of Nārada Muni, who was once asked by a *brāhmaṇa:* "Oh, you are going to meet the Lord? Will you please ask Him when I'm going to get my salvation?"

"All right," Nārada agreed. "I shall ask Him."

As Nārada proceeded, he met a cobbler who was sitting under a tree mending shoes, and the cobbler similarly asked Nārada, "Oh, you are going to see God? Will you please inquire of Him when my salvation will come?"

When Nārada Muni went to the Vaikuṇṭha planets, he fulfilled their request and asked Nārāyaṇa (God) about the salvation of the *brāhmaṇa* and the cobbler, and Nārāyaṇa replied, "After leaving this body, the cobbler shall come here to me."

"What about the *brāhmaṇa*?" Nārada asked.

"He will have to remain there for a number of births. I do not know when he is coming."

Nārada Muni was astonished, and he finally said, "I can't understand the mystery of this."

"That you will see," Nārāyaṇa said. "When they ask you what I am doing in My abode, tell them that I am threading the eye of a needle with an elephant."

When Nārada returned to earth and approached the *brāhmaṇa*, the *brāhmaṇa* said, "Oh, you have seen the Lord? What was He doing?"

"He was threading an elephant through the eye of a needle," Nārada answered.

"I don't believe such nonsense," the *brāhmaṇa* replied. Nārada could immediately understand that the man had no faith and that he was simply a reader of books.

Nārada then left and went on to the cobbler, who asked him, "Oh, you have seen the Lord? Tell me, what was He doing?"

"He was threading an elephant through the eye of a needle," Nārada replied.

The cobbler began to weep, "Oh, my Lord is so wonderful, He can do anything."

"Do you really believe that the Lord can push an elephant through the hole of a needle?" Nārada asked.

"Why not?" the cobbler said, "Of course I believe it."

"How is that?"

"You can see that I am sitting under this banyan tree," the cobbler answered, "and you can see that so many fruits are falling daily, and in each seed there is a banyan tree like this one. If, within a small seed there can be a big tree like this, is it difficult to accept that the Lord is pushing an elephant through the eye of a needle?"

So this is called faith. It is not a question of blindly believing. There is reason behind the belief. If Kṛṣṇa can put a large tree within so many little seeds, is it so astounding that He is keeping all the planetary systems floating in space through His energy?

Although scientists may think that the planets are being held in space simply by nature alone, behind nature there is the Supreme Lord. Nature is acting under His guidance. As Śrī Kṛṣṇa states:

mayādhyakṣeṇa prakṛtiḥ
sūyate sa-carācaram
hetunānena kaunteya
jagad viparivartate

"This material nature is working under My direction, O son of Kuntī, and is producing all moving and unmoving beings. By its rule this manifestation is being created and annihilated again and again." (Bg. 9.10)

Mayādhyakṣeṇa means "under My supervision." Material nature cannot act so wonderfully unless the Lord's hand is behind it. We cannot give any example of material things automatically working. Matter is inert, and without the spiritual touch there is no possibility of its acting. Matter cannot act independently or automatically. Machines may be very wonderfully constructed, but unless a man touches that machine, it cannot work. And what is that man? He is a spiritual spark. Without spiritual touch, nothing can move; therefore everything is resting on Kṛṣṇa's impersonal energy. Kṛṣṇa's energy is impersonal, but He is a person. We often hear of persons performing wonderful actions, yet despite their energetic accomplishments, they still remain persons. If this is possible for human beings, why isn't it possible for the Supreme Lord? We are all persons, but we are all dependent upon Kṛṣṇa, the Supreme Person.

We have often seen pictures of Atlas, a stout man bearing a large planet on his shoulders and struggling very hard to hold it up. We may think that because Kṛṣṇa is maintaining the universe, He is struggling under its burden like Atlas. But this is not the case.

na ca mat-sthāni bhūtāni
paśya me yogam aiśvaram
bhūta-bhṛn na ca bhūta-stho
mamātmā bhūta-bhāvanaḥ

"And yet everything that is created does not rest in Me. Behold My mystic opulence. Although I am the maintainer of all living entities and although I am everywhere, still My Self is the very source of creation." (Bg. 9.5)

Although all beings in the universe are resting in Kṛṣṇa's energy, still they are not in Him. Kṛṣṇa is maintaining all living entities, and His energy is all-pervading, yet He is elsewhere. This is Kṛṣṇa's inconceivable mystic power. He is everywhere, yet He is aloof from everything. We can perceive his energy, but we cannot see Him because He cannot be seen with material eyes. However, when we develop our spiritual qualities, we sanctify our senses so that even within this energy we can see Him. Electricity, for instance, is everywhere, and an electrician is capable of utilizing it. Similarly, the energy of the Supreme Lord is everywhere, and when we become transcendentally situated, we can see God eye to eye everywhere. That spiritualization of the senses is possible through devotional service and love of God. The Lord is all-pervading all over the universe and is within the soul, the heart, water, air–everywhere. Thus if we make an image of God in anything–clay, stone, wood or whatever–it should not be considered to be just a doll. That also is God. If we have sufficient devotion, the image will also speak to us. God is everywhere impersonally *(mayā tatam idaṁ sarvam)*, but if we make His personal form from anything, or if we create an image of God within ourselves, He will be present personally for us. In the *śāstras*, there are eight kinds of images recommended, and any kind of image can be worshiped because God is everywhere. One may protest and ask, "Why should God be worshiped in images and not in His original spiritual form?" The answer is that we cannot see God immediately in His spiritual form. With our material eyes we can only see stone, earth, wood–something tangible. Therefore Kṛṣṇa comes as *arcā-vigraha*, a form conveniently presented by the Supreme Lord in order for us to see Him. The result is that if we concentrate upon the image and make offerings with love and devotion, Kṛṣṇa will respond through the image.

There are many instances of this happening. In India, there is one temple called Sākṣi-Gopāla (Kṛṣṇa is often called Gopāla). The Gopāla *mūrti* or statue was at one time located in a temple in Vṛndāvana. Once two *brāhmaṇas*, one old and one young, went to visit Vṛndāvana on a pilgrimage. It was a long trip, and in those days there were no railways, so travelers underwent many hardships. The old man was much obliged to the youth for helping him on the journey, and upon arriving in Vṛndāvana, he said to him: "My dear boy, you have rendered me so much service, and I am much obliged to you. I would like very much to return that service and give you some reward."

"My dear sir," the youth said, "you are an old man just like my father. It is my duty to serve you. I don't require any reward."

"No, I'm obliged to you, and I must reward you," the old man insisted. He then promised to give the young man his young daughter in marriage.

The old man was a very rich man, and the youth, although a learned *brāhmaṇa,* was very poor. Considering this, the youth said, "Don't promise this, for your family will never agree. I am such a poor man, and you are aristocratic, so this marriage will not take place. Don't promise this way before the Deity."

The conversation was taking place in the temple before the Deity of Gopāla Kṛṣṇa, and the young man was anxious not to offend the Deity. However, despite the youth's pleas, the old man insisted on the marriage. After staying in Vṛndāvana for some time, they finally returned home, and the old man informed his eldest son that his young sister was to be married to the poor *brāhmaṇa* youth. The eldest son became very angry. "Oh, how have you selected that pauper as husband for my sister? This cannot be."

The old man's wife also came to him and said, "If you marry our daughter to that boy, I shall commit suicide."

The old man was thus perplexed. After some time, the *brāhmaṇa* youth became very anxious. "He has promised to marry his daughter to me, and he made that promise before the Deity. Now he is not coming to fulfill it." He then went to see the old man to remind him of his promise.

"You promised before Lord Kṛṣṇa," the youth said, "and you are not fulfilling that promise. How is that?"

The old man was silent. He began praying to Kṛṣṇa, for he was perplexed. He didn't want to marry his daughter to the youth and cause such great trouble within his family. In the meantime the elder son came out and began to accuse the *brāhmaṇa* youth. "You have plundered my father in the place of pilgrimage. You gave him some intoxicant and took all his money, and now you are saying that he has promised to offer you my youngest sister. You rascal!"

In this way there was much noise, and people began to gather. The youth could understand that the old man was still agreeable but that the family was making it difficult for him. People began to gather about because of the noise which the elder son was raising, and the *brāhmaṇa* youth began to exclaim to them that the old man made this promise before the Deities but that he could not fulfill it because the family was objecting. The eldest son, who was an atheist, suddenly interrupted the youth and said, "You say that the Lord was witnessing. Well, if He comes and bears witness to this promise of my father's, you can have my sister in marriage."

The youth replied, "Yes, I shall ask Kṛṣṇa to come as a witness." He was confident that God would come. An agreement was then made before everyone that the girl would be given in marriage if Kṛṣṇa came from Vṛndāvana as a witness to the old man's promise.

The *brāhmaṇa* youth returned to Vṛndāvana and began to pray to Gopāla Kṛṣṇa. "Dear Lord, You must come with me." He was such a staunch devotee that he spoke to Kṛṣṇa just as one would speak to a friend. He was not thinking that the Gopāla was a mere statue or image, but he considered Him to be God Himself. Suddenly the Deity spoke to him:

"How do you think that I can go with you? I am a statue. I can't go anywhere."

"Well, if a statue can speak, he can also walk," the boy replied.

"All right then," the Deity said finally. "I shall go with you, but on one condition. In no case shall you look back to see Me. I will follow you, and you will know that I am following by the jingle of My leg bangles."

The youth agreed, and in this way they left Vṛndāvana to go to the other town. When the trip was nearly over, just as they were about to enter his home village, the youth could no longer hear the sound of the bangles, and he began to fear. "Oh, where is Kṛṣṇa?" Unable to contain himself any longer, he looked back. He saw the statue standing still. Because he looked back, it would go no further. He immediately ran into the town and told the people to come out and see Kṛṣṇa who had come as a witness. Everyone was astounded that such a large statue had come from such a distance, and they built a temple on the spot in honor of the Deity, and today people are still worshiping Sākṣi-Gopāla, the Lord as a witness.

We should therefore conclude that because God is everywhere, He is also in His statue, in the image made of Him. If Kṛṣṇa is everywhere, as even the impersonalists admit, then why isn't He in His image? Whether an image or statue speaks to us or not is dependent on the degree of our devotion. But if we choose to see the image merely as a piece of wood or stone, Kṛṣṇa will always remain wood or stone for us. Kṛṣṇa is everywhere, but as we advance in spiritual consciousness we can begin to see Him as He is. If we put a letter into a mailbox, it will go to its destination because the mailbox is authorized. Similarly, if we worship an authorized image of God, our faith will have some effect. If we are prepared to follow the various rules and regulations—that is to say, if we become qualified—it is possible to see God anywhere and everywhere. When a devotee is present, Kṛṣṇa, by

His omnipresent energies, will manifest Himself anywhere and everywhere, but when His devotee is not there, He will not do this. There are many instances of this. Prahlāda Mahārāja saw Kṛṣṇa in a pillar. There are many other examples. Kṛṣṇa is there; all that is required is our qualification to see Him.

Kṛṣṇa Himself gives an example of His omnipresence in this way:

yathākāśa-sthito nityaṁ
vāyuḥ sarvatra-go mahān
tathā sarvāṇi bhūtāni
mat-sthānīty upadhāraya

"As the mighty wind, blowing everywhere, always rests in ethereal space, know that in the same manner all beings rest in Me." (Bg. 9.6)

Everyone knows that the wind blows within space, and on earth it is blowing everywhere. There is no place where there is no air or wind. If we wish to drive out air, we have to create a vacuum artificially by some machine. Just as the air is blowing everywhere in space, so everything is existing within Kṛṣṇa. If this is the case, when the material creation is dissolved, where does it go?

sarva-bhūtāni kaunteya
prakṛtiṁ yānti māmikām
kalpa-kṣaye punas tāni
kalpādau visṛjāmy aham

"O son of Kuntī, at the end of the millennium every material manifestation enters into My nature, and at the beginning of another millennium, by My potency I again create." (Bg. 9.7)

Kṛṣṇa sets His nature (*prakṛti*) into motion, as one may wind up a clock, and when nature unwinds, it is absorbed into the Lord. The spiritual creation, however, is not like this, for it is permanent. In the material creation everything is temporary. Just as our bodies are developing due to the spiritual spark that is within, the whole creation is coming into being, developing and passing out of being, due to the spirit of the Lord which is within it. Just as our spirit is present within the body, the Lord is present within the universe as Paramātmā. Due to the presence of Kṣīrodakaśāyī Viṣṇu, the material creation exists, just as due to our presence our bodies are existing. Sometimes Kṛṣṇa manifests the material creation, and sometimes He does not. In all cases, its existence is due to His presence.

4

Knowledge by Way of the Mahātmās, Great Souls

The presence of Kṛṣṇa in all aspects of the creation is perceived by the *mahātmās,* the great souls, who are always engaged in the worship of Kṛṣṇa. As Kṛṣṇa Himself states, these great souls are conversant with the confidential knowledge found in the Ninth Chapter of *Bhagavad-gītā,* and they know Kṛṣṇa to be the source of all things.

mahātmānas tu māṁ pārtha
daivīṁ prakṛtim āśritāḥ
bhajanty ananya-manaso
jñātvā bhūtādim avyayam

"O son of Pṛthā, those who are not deluded, the great souls, are under the protection of the divine nature. They are fully engaged in devotional service because they know Me as the Supreme Personality of Godhead, original and inexhaustible." (Bg. 9.13)

The great soul knows without a doubt that Kṛṣṇa is the Supreme Personality of Godhead and that He is the origin of all emanations. The *Vedānta-sūtra* states, *athāto brahma-jijñāsā:* Human life is meant for inquiring about Brahman. At present we are all engaged in studying temporary, small things. Brahman means the greatest, but instead of concerning ourselves with the greatest, we have become enmeshed in trying to solve the animal problems of eating, sleeping, defending and mating. These small problems are automatically solved. Even the animals are enjoying mating, sleeping, eating and defending. The arrangements are all provided. These demands of the body are not really problems, but we have made them into problems. The *Vedānta-sūtra* enjoins us not to concern ourselves with these problems, for they are satisfied in any form of life. Our problem is to inquire about the source of all these manifestations. The human form of life is not meant for struggling hard to solve the material problems which even a hog, a stool-eater, can solve. The hog is considered to be the lowest among animals, yet he has eating facility, mating facility, sleeping facility, and facilities for defense. Even if we don't strive for these things, we will have them. Man is meant, rather, to find out the source from which all these things are coming. The *Vedānta-sūtra* states that Brahman is that from which everything is emanating *(janmādy asya yataḥ).* Philosophers, scientists, *yogīs, jñānīs* and transcendentalists are all trying to find out the ultimate source of everything. This source is given in *Brahma-saṁhitā, sarva-kāraṇa-kāraṇam:* Kṛṣṇa is the cause of all causes.

Understanding Kṛṣṇa to be the primal source of everything, how do the great souls act? Kṛṣṇa Himself characterizes them in this way:

satataṁ kīrtayanto māṁ
yatantaś ca dṛḍha-vratāḥ
namasyantaś ca māṁ bhaktyā
nitya-yuktā upāsate

"Always chanting My glories, endeavoring with great determination, bowing down before Me, these great souls perpetually worship Me with devotion." (Bg. 9.14)

That glorification is this process of *bhakti-yoga*, the chanting of Hare Kṛṣṇa. The great souls, understanding the nature of God, His descent and His mission, glorify Him in so many ways, but there are others who do not accept Him. Kṛṣṇa also mentions them in the Ninth Chapter:

avajānanti māṁ mūḍhā
mānuṣīṁ tanum āśritam
paraṁ bhāvam ajānanto
mama bhūta-maheśvaram

"Fools deride Me when I descend in the human form. They do not know My transcendental nature and my supreme dominion over all that be." (Bg. 9.11)

The *mūḍhas*, or foolish men, who are lower than the animals, deride Him. Any person who doesn't believe in God must either be a madman or fool number one. There is no reason not to believe in God, and there is every reason to believe in Him. Man may say that he doesn't believe in God, but who gives him the power to say this? When death comes, this speaking power ceases—so who is giving the power of speech? Has the speaking power come automatically from stone? As soon as the speaking power is withdrawn by the Supreme Authority, the body is no better than stone. The very power of speech is proof that there is a Supreme Power who is giving us everything. A Kṛṣṇa conscious person knows that whatever he has is not under his control. If we do not believe in God, we must believe in some power beyond us which is controlling us at every step, call that power God or nature or whatever. There is a controlling power in the universe, and no sane man can deny it.

Kṛṣṇa was present on this earth and appeared just like a human being with supernatural power. At that time, however, ninety-nine percent of the people could not recognize Him as God. They could not recognize Him because they had no eyes to see *(paraṁ bhāvam ajānantaḥ)*. How is it possible to recognize God? He can be recognized through supernatural power, by the evidence of authorities, and by scriptural evidence. As far as Kṛṣṇa is concerned, every Vedic authority has accepted Him as God. When He was present on earth, His activities displayed were superhuman. If one does not believe this, it is to be concluded that he will not believe whatever evidence is given.

One must also have the eyes to see God. God cannot be seen by material senses, therefore the *bhakti-yoga* process is the process of purifying the senses so that we will be able to understand what and who God is. We have power of seeing, hearing, touching, tasting and so on, but if these senses are blunt, we cannot understand God. The process of Kṛṣṇa consciousness is the process of training these senses through regulated principles, specifically through the chanting of Hare Kṛṣṇa.

Śrī Kṛṣṇa further characterizes the *mūḍhas:*

moghāśā mogha-karmāṇo
mogha-jñānā vicetasaḥ
rākṣasīm āsurīṁ caiva
prakṛtiṁ mohinīṁ śritāḥ

"Those who are thus bewildered are attracted by demonic and atheistic views. In that deluded condition, their hopes for liberation, their fruitive activities, and their culture of knowledge are all defeated." (Bg. 9.12)

The word *moghāśa* indicates that the aspirations of the atheists will be baffled. The *karmīs,* or fruitive laborers, are always hoping for something better to gratify their senses. There is no limit to where they will stop. They are trying to increase their bank balance and are hoping to be happy at a certain point, but that point never comes because they do not know the ultimate point of satiation. Those who are enamored by the attractions of illusory energy cannot understand the ultimate aim of life. The word *mogha-karmāṇaḥ* indicates that they are laboring very hard but that in the end they will only meet with frustration. Unless we are established in Kṛṣṇa consciousness, all of our activities will be baffled at the end.

This is not the verdict of an ordinary man, but of Śrī Kṛṣṇa Himself. If we are searching for knowledge, we should conduct research to find out whether Kṛṣṇa is *not* God. Without any objective, what is the point of thousands of years of speculation? The Supreme Lord is so vast that one cannot reach Him by mental speculation. If we travel at the speed of mind and wind for millions of years, it is not possible to reach the Supreme by speculation. There is not one single instance in which one has arrived at the Supreme Absolute Truth by means of his own mental speculation. Therefore the word *mogha-jñānāḥ* indicates that the process of mundane knowledge is bewildering. Through our own endeavor it is not possible to see the sun after it has set. We have to wait until the sun reveals itself in the morning at sunrise. If it is not possible with our limited senses to perceive a material thing like the sun, how is it possible to perceive the nonmaterial? We cannot find out or understand Kṛṣṇa by our own endeavor. We have to qualify ourselves through Kṛṣṇa consciousness and wait for Him to reveal Himself.

teṣāṁ satata-yuktānāṁ
bhajatāṁ prīti-pūrvakam
dadāmi buddhi-yogaṁ taṁ
yena mām upayānti te

"To those who are constantly devoted and worship Me with love, I give the understanding by which they can come to Me." (Bg. 10.10)

Kṛṣṇa is within, but due to our material conditioning, we do not realize it. Those who are of the nature of fiends and demons *(rākṣasīm āsurīm)* think that this material life is all and that it is the purpose of human life to squeeze out as much pleasure from matter as possible. They try squeezing, but they are constantly baffled. Squeezing material nature is not the process for finding out real pleasure. If we are searching for real pleasure, we have to take to Kṛṣṇa consciousness. All happiness in the material world has a beginning and an end, but happiness in Kṛṣṇa is unlimited, and there is no end. In order to get this happiness we simply have to sacrifice a little time and chant Hare Kṛṣṇa. In former ages, the great sages and demigods used to sacrifice their whole lives for realizing the Supreme, and still they would not attain success. For this age Caitanya Mahāprabhu has given an easy process for God realization. All that is necessary is careful listening. We have to listen to *Bhagavad-gītā,* and we have to chant the names of Kṛṣṇa and listen to them carefully. We should not be puffed up, falsely thinking that our knowledge is great or that we are very learned. We need only become a little gentle and submissive to hear the messages from Kṛṣṇa.

At present, this world is being managed by the *rākṣasas.* The *rākṣasas* are man-eaters who eat their own sons for the satisfaction of their senses. Now great regimes have been created to smash so many people for the satisfaction of the *rākṣasas* senses, but they do not realize that their senses will never be satisfied in this way. Nonetheless, the *rākṣasas* are prepared to sacrifice everything to satisfy their whimsical desires. It is very difficult for them to understand the real situation because they are overly enamored with material civilization. Who then can understand? Those who are *mahātmās,* whose hearts have become magnified, understand that "everything belongs to God, and I also belong to God."

Such *mahātmās* are not under the control of material nature *(mahātmānas tu māṁ pārtha daivīṁ prakṛtim āśritāḥ).* God is great and the *mahātmā's* heart also becomes great by serving the great. *Mahātmā* is not a stamp for a political leader. One cannot be stamped *mahātmā* by votes. The standard for *mahātmā* is given in *Bhagavad-gītā:* the *mahātmā* is he who has taken shelter of the superior energy of the Lord. Of course all energies are His, and He does not make distinctions between spiritual energy and material energy, but for the conditioned soul who is situated marginally between material energy and spiritual energy, there is a distinction. The *mahātmās* see this distinction and so take shelter under the spiritual energy *(daivīṁ prakṛtim).*

By serving the great, the *mahātmās* also become great through identifying with the superior energy: *(ahaṁ brahmāsmi)* "I am Brahman—spirit." It is not that they become puffed up and think that they are God. Rather, if one becomes Brahman, he must show his activities in Brahman. Spirit is active, and to become Brahman is not to become inactive. Brahman is spirit, and these material bodies are active only because Brahman is within them. If we are active despite our contact with material nature, do we cease to be active when we purify ourselves of the material contamination and establish ourselves in our proper identity as pure Brahman? Realizing "I am Brahman" means engagement in spiritual activity because we are spirit, and our activities are exhibited even though we are contaminated by matter. To become Brahman does not mean to become void but to establish ourselves in the superior nature, which means superior energy and superior activities. To become Brahman means to be completely engaged in rendering devotional service to the Lord. Thus the *mahātmā* understands that if service is to be rendered, it is to be to Kṛṣṇa and no one else. We have so long served our senses; now we should serve Kṛṣṇa.

There is no question of stopping service, for we are meant for service. Is there anyone who does not serve? If we ask the President, "Who are you serving?" he will tell us that he is serving the country. No one is devoid of service. Service we cannot stop, but we do have to redirect our service from the illusion to the reality. When this is done, we become *mahātmā.*

This process of *kīrtana (kīrtayantaḥ),* always chanting the glories of the Lord, is the beginning of *mahātmā.* That process is simplified by Lord Caitanya Mahāprabhu who imparted to mankind this chanting of Hare Kṛṣṇa, Hare Kṛṣṇa, Kṛṣṇa Kṛṣṇa, Hare Hare/ Hare Rāma, Hare Rāma, Rāma Rāma, Hare Hare. There are nine different processes of devotional service, of which *śravaṇaṁ kīrtanam,* hearing and chanting, are the most important. *Kīrtanam* actually means "describing." We can describe with music, words, pictures, etc. *Śravaṇam* goes hand in hand with *kīrtanam,* for unless we hear, we cannot describe. We don't need any material qualifications in order to attain the Supreme. All we have to do is hear from authoritative sources and repeat accurately what we hear.

Formerly, the *Vedas* were heard by the student from the spiritual master, and thus the *Vedas* became known as *śruti,* meaning "that which is heard."

In *Bhagavad-gītā,* for example, we see that Arjuna is listening to Kṛṣṇa on the battlefield. He is not engaged in the study of *Vedānta* philosophy. We can hear from the Supreme Authority in any place, even in the battlefield. The knowledge is received, not manufactured. Some people think, "Why should I listen to Him? I can think for myself. I can manufacture something new." This is not the Vedic process of descending knowledge. By ascending knowledge, one tries to elevate himself by his own effort, but by descending knowledge one receives the knowledge from a superior source. In the Vedic tradition, knowledge is imparted to the student from the spiritual master, as in *Bhagavad-gītā (evaṁ paramparā-prāptam imaṁ rājarṣayo viduḥ).* Submissive hearing is so powerful that simply by hearing from authoritative sources we can become completely perfect. In becoming submissive, we become aware of our own imperfections. As long as we are conditioned, we are subject to four kinds of imperfections: we are sure to commit mistakes, to become illusioned, to have imperfect senses and to cheat. Therefore our attempt to understand the Absolute Truth by our faulty senses and experience is futile. We must hear from a representative of Kṛṣṇa who is a devotee of Kṛṣṇa's. Kṛṣṇa made Arjuna His representative because Arjuna was His devotee: *bhakto 'si me sakhā ceti.* (Bg. 4.3)

No one can become a representative of God without being a devotee of God's. One who thinks, "I am God," cannot be a representative. Because we are part and parcel of God, our qualities are the same as

His, and therefore if we study these qualities in ourselves, we come to learn something of God. This does not mean that we understand the quantity of God. This self-realization process is one way of understanding God, but in no case can we preach, "I am God." We cannot claim to be God without being able to display the powers of God. As far as Kṛṣṇa is concerned, He proved that He was God by displaying so much power and by revealing His universal form to Arjuna. Kṛṣṇa showed this awesome form in order to discourage people who would claim to be God. We should not be fooled by one who claims to be God; following in the footsteps of Arjuna, we should request to see the universal form before accepting anyone as God. Only a fool would accept another fool as God.

No one can be equal to God, and no one can be above Him. Even Lord Brahmā and Śiva, the most exalted demigods, are subservient to Him and pay their respectful obeisances. Instead of trying to become God by some meditational process or other, we had better hear about God submissively and try to understand Him and our relationship to Him. The representative of God or the incarnation of God never claims to be God but the servant of God. This is the sign of the bona fide representative.

Whatever we learn of God from authoritative sources can be described, and that will help us make spiritual progress. This description is called *kīrtana.* If we try to repeat what we hear, we become established in knowledge. By the process of *śravaṇaṁ kīrtanam,* hearing and chanting, we can become free from material conditioning and attain to the kingdom of God. In this age it is impossible to practice sacrifice, speculation or *yoga.* There is no way open to us but the way of hearing submissively from authoritative sources. This is the way the *mahātmās* received the most confidential knowledge. It is the way Arjuna received it from Kṛṣṇa, and it is the way we must receive it from the disciplic succession stemming from Arjuna.

5

Paramparā: Knowledge Through Disciplic Succession

śrī bhagavān uvāca
imaṁ vivasvate yogaṁ
proktavān aham avyayam
vivasvān manave prāha
manur ikṣvākave 'bravīt

"The Blessed Lord said: I instructed this imperishable science of *yoga* to the sun-god, Vivasvān, and Vivasvān instructed it to Manu, the father of mankind, and Manu in turn instructed it to Ikṣvāku." (Bg. 4.1)

Many ages ago Kṛṣṇa imparted the divine knowledge of *Bhagavad-gītā* to Vivasvān, the god of the sun. To the best of our knowledge, the sun is a very hot place, and we do not consider it possible for anyone to live there. It is not even possible to approach the sun very closely with these bodies. However, from the Vedic literatures we can understand that the sun is a planet just like this one but that everything there is composed of fire. Just as this planet is predominately composed of earth, there are other planets which are predominately composed of fire, water and air.

The living entities on these various planets acquire bodies composed of elements in accordance with the predominating element on the planet; therefore those beings who live on the sun have bodies which are composed of fire. Of all beings on the sun, the principal personality is a god by the name of Vivasvān. He is known as the sun-god (*sūrya-nārāyaṇa*). On all planets there are principal personalities, just as in the United States the chief person is the President. From the history called the *Mahābhārata* we understand that formerly there was only one king on this planet by the name of Mahārāja Bharata. He ruled some 5,000 years ago, and the planet was named after him. Subsequently the earth has become divided into so many different countries. In this way there is usually one and sometimes many controllers of the various planets in the universe.

From this first verse of the Fourth Chapter we learn that millions of years ago Śrī Kṛṣṇa imparted the knowledge of *karma-yoga* to the sun god Vivasvān. Śrī Kṛṣṇa, who imparts the teachings of *Bhagavad-gītā* to Arjuna, here indicates that these teachings are not at all new but were enunciated many ages ago on a different planet. Vivasvān, in his turn, repeated these teachings to his son, Manu. In turn, Manu imparted the knowledge to his disciple Ikṣvāku. Mahārāja Ikṣvāku was a great king and forefather of Lord Rāmacandra. The point being made here is that if one wants to learn *Bhagavad-gītā* and profit by it, there is a process for understanding it, and that process is described here. It is not that Kṛṣṇa is speaking *Bhagavad-gītā* to Arjuna for the first time. It is estimated by Vedic authorities that the Lord imparted these divine instructions to Vivasvān some 400 million years ago. From the

Mahābhārata we understand that *Bhagavad-gītā* was spoken to Arjuna some 5,000 years ago. Before Arjuna, the teachings were handed down by disciplic succession, but over such a long period of time, the teachings became lost.

evaṁ paramparā-prāptam
imaṁ rājarṣayo viduḥ
sa kāleneha mahatā
yogo naṣṭaḥ parantapa

sa evāyaṁ mayā te 'dya
yogaḥ proktaḥ purātanaḥ
bhakto 'si me sakhā ceti
rahasyaṁ hy etad uttamam

"This supreme science was thus received through the chain of disciplic succession, and the saintly kings understood it in that way. But in course of time the succession was broken, and therefore the science as it is appears to be lost. That very ancient science of the relationship with the Supreme is today told by Me to you because you are My devotee as well as My friend; therefore you can understand the transcendental mystery of this science." (Bg. 4.2-3)

In *Bhagavad-gītā* a number of *yoga* systems are delineated—*bhakti-yoga, karma-yoga, jñāna-yoga, haṭha-yoga*—and therefore it is here called *yoga.* The word *yoga* means "to link up," and the idea is that in *yoga* we link our consciousness to God. It is a means for reuniting with God or re-establishing our relationship with Him. In the course of time, this *yoga* imparted by Śrī Kṛṣṇa was lost. Why is this? Were there no learned sages at the time Śrī Kṛṣṇa was speaking to Arjuna? No, there were many sages present at the time. By "lost" it is meant that the purport of *Bhagavad-gītā* was lost. Scholars may give their own interpretation of *Bhagavad-gītā*, analyzing it according to their own whims, but that is not *Bhagavad-gītā.* This is the point that Śrī Kṛṣṇa is stressing, and a student of *Bhagavad-gītā* should note it. A person may be a very good scholar from the material point of view, but that does not qualify him to comment on *Bhagavad-gītā.* In order to understand *Bhagavad-gītā,* we have to accept the principle of disciplic succession (*paramparā*). We must enter into the spirit of *Bhagavad-gītā* and not approach it simply from the viewpoint of erudition.

Of all people, why did Śrī Kṛṣṇa select Arjuna as a recipient of this knowledge? Arjuna was not a great scholar at all, nor was he a *yogī,* meditator or a holy man. He was a warrior about to engage in battle. There were many great sages living at the time, and Śrī Kṛṣṇa could have given *Bhagavad-gītā* to them. The answer is that despite being an ordinary man, Arjuna had one great qualification: *bhakto 'si me sakhā ceti:* "You are My devotee and My friend." This was Arjuna's exceptional qualification, a qualification which the sages did not have. Arjuna knew that Kṛṣṇa was the Supreme Personality of Godhead, and therefore he surrendered himself unto Him, accepting Him as his spiritual master. Unless one is a devotee of Lord Kṛṣṇa's, he cannot possibly understand *Bhagavad-gītā.* If one wants to understand *Bhagavad-gītā,* he cannot take help from other methods. He must understand it as prescribed in *Bhagavad-gītā* itself, by understanding it as Arjuna understood it. If we wish to understand *Bhagavad-gītā* in a different way, or give an individual interpretation, that may be an exhibition of our scholarship, but it is not *Bhagavad-gītā.*

By scholarship we may be able to manufacture some theory of *Bhagavad-gītā,* just as Mahātmā Gandhi did when he interpreted *Bhagavad-gītā* in an effort to support his theory of nonviolence. How is it possible to prove nonviolence from *Bhagavad-gītā?* The very theme of *Bhagavad-gītā* involves Arjuna's reluctance to fight and Kṛṣṇa's inducing him to kill his opponents. In fact, Kṛṣṇa tells Arjuna that the battle had already been decided by the Supreme, that the people who were assembled on the battlefield were predestined never to return. It was Kṛṣṇa's program that the warriors were all destined to die, and Kṛṣṇa gave Arjuna the opportunity of taking the credit of conquering them. If fighting is proclaimed a necessity in *Bhagavad-gītā,* how is it possible to prove nonviolence from it? Such interpretations are attempts to distort *Bhagavad-gītā.* As soon as the *Gītā* is interpreted according to the motive of an individual, the purpose is lost. It is stated that we cannot attain the conclusion of the Vedic literature by the force of our own logic or argument. There are many things which do not come within the jurisdiction of our sense of logic. As far as scriptures are concerned, we find different scriptures describing the Absolute Truth in different ways. If we analyze all of them, there will be bewilderment.

There are also many philosophers with different opinions, and they're always contradicting one another. If the truth cannot be understood by reading various scriptures, by logical argument or philosophical theories, then how can it be attained? The fact is that the wisdom of the Absolute Truth is very confidential, but if we follow the authorities, it can be understood.

In India, there are disciplic successions coming from Rāmānujācārya, Madhvācārya, Nimbārka, Viṣṇusvāmī and other great sages. The Vedic literatures are understood through the superior spiritual masters. Arjuna understood *Bhagavad-gītā* from Kṛṣṇa, and if we wish to understand it, we have to understand it from Arjuna, not from any other source. If we have any knowledge of *Bhagavad-gītā*, we have to see how it tallies with the understanding of Arjuna. If we understand *Bhagavad-gītā* in the same way that Arjuna did, we should know that our understanding is correct. This should be the criteria for our studying of *Bhagavad-gītā*. If we actually want to receive benefit from *Bhagavad-gītā*, we have to follow this principle. *Bhagavad-gītā* is not an ordinary book of knowledge which we can purchase from the market place, read and merely consult a dictionary to understand. This is not possible. If it were, Kṛṣṇa would never have told Arjuna that the science was lost.

It is not difficult to understand the necessity of going through the disciplic succession to understand *Bhagavad-gītā*. If we wish to be a lawyer, an engineer or doctor, we have to receive knowledge from the authoritative lawyers, engineers and doctors. A new lawyer has to become an apprentice of an experienced lawyer, or a young man studying to be a doctor has to become an intern and work with those who are already licensed practitioners. Our knowledge of a subject cannot be perfectionalized unless we receive it through authoritative sources.

There are two processes for attaining knowledge—one is inductive and the other is deductive. The deductive method is considered to be more perfect. We may take a premise such as, "All men are mortal," and no one need discuss how man is mortal. It is generally accepted that this is the case. The deductive conclusion is: "Mr. Johnson is a man; therefore Mr. Johnson is mortal." But how is the premise that all men are mortal arrived at? Followers of the inductive method wish to arrive at this premise through experiment and observations. We may thus study that this man died and that man died, etc., and after seeing that so many men have died we may conclude or generalize that all men are mortal, but there is a major defect in this inductive method, and that is that our experience is limited. We may never have seen a man who is not mortal, but we are judging this on our personal experience, which is finite. Our senses have limited power, and there are so many defects in our conditional state. The inductive process consequently is not always perfect, whereas the deductive process from a source of perfect knowledge is perfect. The Vedic process is such a process.

Although the authority is acknowledged, there are many passages in *Bhagavad-gītā* which appear to be dogmatic. For instance, in the Seventh Chapter Śrī Kṛṣṇa says:

mattaḥ parataraṁ nānyat
kiñcid asti dhanañjaya
mayi sarvam idaṁ protaṁ
sūtre maṇi-gaṇā iva

"O conqueror of wealth (Arjuna), there is no Truth superior to Me. Everything rests upon Me, as pearls are strung on a thread." (Bg. 7.7)

Śrī Kṛṣṇa is saying that there is no authority greater than Him, and this appears to be very dogmatic. If I say, "There is no one greater than me," people would think, "Oh, Svāmījī is very proud." If a man who is conditioned by so many imperfections says that he is the greatest of all, he blasphemes. But Kṛṣṇa can say this, for we can understand from the histories that even while He was on this earth, He was considered the greatest personality of His time. Indeed, He was the greatest in all fields of activity.

According to the Vedic system, knowledge which is achieved from the greatest authority is to be considered perfect. According to the *Vedas,* there are three kinds of proof: *pratyakṣa, anumāna* and *śabda.* One is by direct visual perception. If a person is sitting in front of me, I can see him sitting there, and my knowledge of his sitting there is received through my eyes. The second method, *anumāna,* is auricular: we may hear children playing outside, and by hearing we can conjecture that they are there. And the third method is the method of taking truths from a higher authority. Such a saying as "Man is mortal" is accepted from higher authorities. Everyone accepts this, but no one has experienced that all men are mortal. By tradition, we have to accept this. If someone asks, "Who found this truth first? Did you discover it?" it is very difficult to say. All we can say is that the knowledge is coming down and that we accept it. Out of the three methods of acquiring knowledge, the *Vedas* say that the third method, that of receiving knowledge from higher authorities, is the most perfect. Direct perception is always imperfect, especially in the conditional stage of life. By direct perception we can see that the sun is just like a disc, no larger than the plate we eat on. From scientists, however, we come to understand that the sun is many thousands of times larger than the earth. So what are we to accept? Are we to accept the scientific proclamation, the proclamation of authorities, or our own experience? Although we cannot ourselves prove how large the sun is, we accept the verdict of astronomers. In this way we are accepting the statements of authorities in every field of our activities. From newspapers and radio we also understand that such and such events are taking place in China and India and other places all around the earth. We're not experiencing these events directly, and we don't know that such events are actually taking place, but we accept the authority of the newspapers and radio. We have no choice but to believe authorities in order to get knowledge. And when the authority is perfect, our knowledge is perfect.

According to the Vedic sources, of all authorities Kṛṣṇa is the greatest and most perfect *(mattaḥ paratarаṁ nānyat kiñcid asti dhanañjaya).* Not only does Kṛṣṇa proclaim Himself to be the highest authority, but this is also accepted by great sages and scholars of *Bhagavad-gītā.* If we do not accept Kṛṣṇa as authority and take His words as they are, we cannot derive any benefit from *Bhagavad-gītā.* It is not dogmatic; it is a fact. If we study scrutinizingly what Kṛṣṇa says, we will find that it is right. Even scholars like Śaṅkarācārya, who have different opinions from the Personality of Godhead, admit that Kṛṣṇa is *svayaṁ bhagavān*—Kṛṣṇa is the Supreme Lord.

Vedic knowledge is not a recent discovery. It is all old revealed knowledge. Kṛṣṇa refers to it as *purātanaḥ,* which means ancient. Kṛṣṇa says that millions of years before He spoke this *yoga* to the sun god, and we do not know how many millions of years before that He spoke it to someone else. This knowledge is always being repeated, just as summer, autumn, winter and spring are repeated every year. Our fund of knowledge is very poor; we do not even know the history of this planet more than 5,000 years back, but the Vedic literatures give us histories extending millions of years ago. Just because we have no knowledge of what happened 3,000 years ago on this planet, we cannot conclude that there was no history then. Of course one can disclaim the historical validity of Kṛṣṇa. One may say that Kṛṣṇa, according to *Mahābhārata,* lived 5,000 years ago, and this being the case, there is no possibility of His having spoken *Bhagavad-gītā* to the sun god so many millions of years before. If I said that I gave a speech on the sun some millions of years ago to the sun god, people would say, "Svāmījī is speaking some nonsense." But this is not the case with Kṛṣṇa, for He is the Supreme Personality of Godhead. Whether we believe that Kṛṣṇa spoke *Bhagavad-gītā* to the sun god or not, this fact is being accepted by Arjuna. Arjuna accepted Kṛṣṇa as the Supreme Lord, and therefore he knew that it was quite possible for Kṛṣṇa to have spoken to someone millions of years before. Although Arjuna personally accepts the statements of Śrī Kṛṣṇa, in order to clarify the situation for people who would come after him, he asks:

aparaṁ bhavato janma
paraṁ janma vivasvataḥ
katham etad vijānīyāṁ
tvam ādau proktavān iti

"The sun-god Vivasvān is senior by birth to You. How am I to understand that in the beginning You instructed this science to him?" (Bg. 4.4)

Actually this is a very intelligent question, and Kṛṣṇa answers it in this way:

bahūni me vyatītāni
janmāni tava cārjuna
tāny ahaṁ veda sarvāṇi
na tvaṁ vettha parantapa

"Many, many births both you and I have passed. I can remember all of them, but you cannot, O subduer of the enemy!" (Bg. 4.5)

Although Kṛṣṇa is God, He incarnates many, many times. Arjuna, being a living entity, also takes his birth many, many times. The difference between the Supreme Personality of Godhead and a living entity is, *tāny ahaṁ veda sarvāṇi:* Kṛṣṇa remembers the events of His past incarnations, whereas the living entity cannot remember. That is one of the differences between God and man. God is eternal, and we are also eternal, but the difference is that we are always changing our bodies. At death we forget the events of our lifetime; death means forgetfulness, that's all. At night, when we go to sleep, we forget that we are the husband of such and such a wife and the father of such and such children. We forget ourselves in sleep, but when we wake up, we remember, "Oh, I am so and so, and I must do such and such." It is a fact that in our previous lives we had other bodies with other families, fathers, mothers and so on in other countries, but we have forgotten all of these. We might have been dogs or cats or men or gods—whatever we were we have now forgotten.

Despite all these changes, as living entities, we are eternal. Just as in previous lives we have prepared for this body, in this lifetime we are preparing for another body. We get our bodies according to our *karma,* or activities. Those who are in the mode of goodness are promoted to higher planets, in a higher status of life (Bg. 14.14). Those who die in the mode of passion remain on earth, and those who die in the mode of ignorance may fall into the animal species of life or may be transferred to a lower planet (Bg. 14.15). This is the process that has been going on, but we forget it.

At one time, Indra, the king of heaven, committed an offense at the feet of his spiritual master, and his spiritual master cursed him to take the birth of a hog. Thus the throne of the heavenly kingdom became empty as Indra went to earth to become a hog. Seeing the situation, Brahmā came to earth and addressed the hog: "My dear sir, you have become a hog on this planet earth. I have come to deliver you. Come with me at once." But the hog replied: "Oh I cannot go with you. I have so many responsibilities—my children, wife and this nice hog society." Even though Brahmā promised to take him back to heaven, Indra, in the form of a hog, refused. This is called forgetfulness. Similarly, Lord Śrī Kṛṣṇa comes and says to us, "What are you doing in this material world? *Sarva-dharmān parityajya mām ekaṁ śaraṇaṁ vraja.* Come to Me, and I'll give you all protection." But we say, "I don't believe You Sir. I have more important business here." This is the position of the conditioned soul—forgetfulness. This forgetfulness is quickly dissipated by following in the path of disciplic succession.

6

Knowledge of Kṛṣṇa's Appearances and Activities

There are two forces of nature working in us. By one we decide that in this lifetime we will make spiritual advancement, but at the next moment the other force, *māyā,* or illusory energy, says, "What is all this trouble that you're going to? Just enjoy this life and be easy with yourself." This tendency to fall into forgetfulness is the difference between God and man. Arjuna is a companion and associate of Kṛṣṇa's, and whenever Kṛṣṇa appears on any planet, Arjuna also takes birth and appears with Him. When Kṛṣṇa spoke *Bhagavad-gītā* to the sun god, Arjuna was also present with Him. But, being a finite living entity, Arjuna could not remember. Forgetfulness is the nature of the living entity. We cannot even remember what we were doing at this exact time yesterday or a week ago. If we cannot remember this, how is it possible to remember what happened in our previous lives? At this point we may ask how it is that Kṛṣṇa can remember and we cannot, and the answer is that Kṛṣṇa does not change His body.

ajo 'pi sann avyayātmā
bhūtānām īśvaro 'pi san
prakṛtiṁ svām adhiṣṭhāya
sambhavāmy ātma-māyayā

"Although I am unborn and My transcendental body never deteriorates, and although I am the Lord of all sentient beings, I still appear in every millennium in My original transcendental form." (Bg. 4.6)

The word *ātma-māyayā* means that Kṛṣṇa descends as He is. He does not change His body, but we, as conditioned souls, change ours, and because of this we forget. Kṛṣṇa knows not only the past, present and future of His activities, but the past, present and future of everyone's activities.

vedāhaṁ samatītāni
vartamānāni cārjuna
bhaviṣyāṇi ca bhūtāni
māṁ tu veda na kaścana

"O Arjuna, as the Supreme Personality of Godhead, I know everything that has happened in the past, all that is happening in the present, and all things that are yet to come. I also know all living entities; but Me no one knows." (Bg. 7.26)

In *Śrīmad-Bhāgavatam* we also find that the Supreme Lord is defined as one who knows everything. This is not the case with even the most elevated living entities, such as Brahmā and Śiva. Only Viṣṇu or Kṛṣṇa knows everything. We may also ask that if the Lord does not change His body, why does He come as an incarnation? There is much difference among philosophers concerning this question. Some say that Kṛṣṇa assumes a material body when He comes, but this is not the case. If He assumed a material body like ours, He could not remember, for forgetfulness is due to the material body. The actual conclusion is that He doesn't change His body. God is called all-powerful, and in the verse quoted above, His omnipotence is explained. Kṛṣṇa has no birth, and He is eternal. Similarly, the living entity has no birth, and he is also eternal. It is only the body with which the living entity identifies that takes birth.

In the very beginning of *Bhagavad-gītā,* in the Second Chapter, Kṛṣṇa explains that what we accept as birth and death is due to the body, and as soon as we regain our spiritual body and get out of the contamination of birth and death, we should be qualitatively as good as Kṛṣṇa. That is the whole process of Kṛṣṇa consciousness—the revival of our original *sac-cid-ānanda* spiritual body. That body is eternal *(sat),* full of knowledge *(cit),* and blissful *(ānanda).* This material body is neither *sat, cit,* nor *ānanda.* It is perishable, whereas the person who is occupying the body is imperishable. It is also full of ignorance, and because it is ignorant and temporary, it is full of misery. We feel severe hot or severe cold due to the material body, but as soon as we revive our spiritual body, we become unaffected by dualities. Even while within the material bodies there are *yogīs* who are impervious to dualities such as heat and cold. As we begin to make spiritual advancement while in the material body, we begin to take on the qualities of a spiritual body. If we put iron into a fire, it becomes hot, and then it becomes red-hot, and finally it is no longer iron, but fire—whatever it touches bursts into flames. As we become advanced in Kṛṣṇa consciousness, our material body will become spiritualized and will no longer be affected by material contamination.

Kṛṣṇa's birth, His appearance and disappearance, are likened unto the appearance and disappearance of the sun. In the morning it appears as if the sun is born from the eastern horizon, but actually it is not. The sun is neither rising nor setting; it is as it is in its position. All risings and settings are due to the rotation of the earth. Similarly, in Vedic literatures there are prescribed schedules for the appearance and disappearance of Śrī Kṛṣṇa. Kṛṣṇa's rising is just like the sun. The sun's rising and setting are going on at every moment; somewhere in the world people are witnessing sunrise and sunset. It is not that at one point Kṛṣṇa is born and at another point He is gone. He is always there somewhere, but He appears to come and go. Kṛṣṇa appears and disappears in many universes. We only have experience of this one universe, but from Vedic literatures we can understand that this universe is but a part of the infinite manifestations of the Supreme Lord.

Although Kṛṣṇa is the Supreme Lord and is unborn and unchangeable, He appears in His original transcendental nature. The word *prakṛti* means "nature." In the Seventh Chapter of *Bhagavad-gītā*, it is stated that there are many kinds of nature. These have been categorized into three basic types. There is external nature, internal nature and marginal nature. The external nature is the manifestation of this material world, and in the Seventh Chapter of *Bhagavad-gītā* this is described as *aparā* or material nature. When Kṛṣṇa appears, He accepts the higher nature *(prakṛtiṁ svām),* not the inferior material nature. Sometimes the head of a state may go to the prison house in order to inspect the prison and see the inmates there, but the prisoners are in error if they think, "The head of the state has come to prison, so he is a prisoner just like us." As pointed out before, Śrī Kṛṣṇa states that fools deride Him when He descends in human form (Bg. 9.11).

Kṛṣṇa, as the Supreme Lord, can come here at any time, and we cannot object and say that He cannot come. He is fully independent, and He can come and disappear as He likes. If the head of a state goes to visit a prison, we are not to assume that he is forced to do so. Kṛṣṇa comes with a purpose, and that is to reclaim fallen conditioned souls. We do not love Kṛṣṇa, but Kṛṣṇa loves us. He claims everyone as His son.

sarva-yoniṣu kaunteya
mūrtayaḥ sambhavanti yāḥ
tāsāṁ brahma mahad yonir
ahaṁ bīja-pradaḥ pitā

"It should be understood that all species of life, O son of Kuntī, are made possible by birth in this material nature, and that I am the seed-giving Father."(Bg. 14.4)

The father is always affectionate to the son. The son may forget the father, but the father can never forget the son. Kṛṣṇa comes to the material universe out of His love for us to deliver us from the miseries of birth and death. He says, "My dear sons, why are you rotting in this miserable world? Come to Me, and I'll give you all protection." We are sons of the Supreme, and we can enjoy life very supremely without any misery and without any doubt. Therefore we should not think that Kṛṣṇa comes here just as we do, being obliged by the laws of nature. The Sanskrit word *avatāra* literally means "he who descends." One who descends from the spiritual universe into the material universe through his own will is called an *avatāra.* Sometimes Śrī Kṛṣṇa descends Himself, and sometimes He sends His representative. The major religions of the world—Christian, Hindu, Buddhist and Moslem—believe in some supreme authority or personality coming down from the kingdom of God. In the Christian religion, Jesus Christ claimed to be the son of God and to be coming from the kingdom of God to reclaim conditioned souls. As followers of *Bhagavad-gītā,* we admit this claim to be true. So basically there is no difference of opinion. In details there may be differences due to differences in culture, climate and people, but the basic principle remains the same—that is, God or His representatives come to reclaim conditioned souls.

yadā yadā hi dharmasya
glānir bhavati bhārata
abhyutthānam adharmasya
tadātmānam sṛjāmy aham

"Whenever and wherever there is a decline in religious practice, O descendant of Bharata, and a predominant rise of irreligion—at that time I descend Myself." (Bg. 4.7)

God is very compassionate. He wishes to see our miseries cease, but we are trying to adjust to these miseries. Because we are part and parcel of the Supreme Lord, we are not meant for these miseries, but somehow or other we have voluntarily accepted them. There are miseries arising from the body and mind, from other living entities and from natural catastrophes. We are either suffering from all three of these miseries, or at least from one. We are always trying to make a solution to these miseries, and this attempt constitutes our struggle for existence. That solution cannot be made by our tiny brain. It can be made only when we take to the shelter of the Supreme Lord.

We can become happy when we are reinstated in our constitutional position, and *Bhagavad-gītā* is meant to reinstate us in that position. God and His representative also come to help. As stated previously, they descend upon the material world from the superior nature and are not subject to the laws of birth, old age, disease and death. Kṛṣṇa gives Arjuna the following reasons for His descent upon the world:

paritrāṇāya sādhūnāṁ
vināśāya ca duṣkṛtām
dharma-saṁsthāpanārthāya
sambhavāmi yuge yuge

"In order to deliver the pious and to annihilate the miscreants, as well as to re-establish the principles of religion, I advent Myself millennium after millennium." (Bg. 4.8)

Here Kṛṣṇa says that He comes when there is a decline in *dharma.* The Sanskrit word *dharma* has been translated into English as "faith," but faith has come to mean a religious system that goes under the name of Christian, Moslem, Hindu, Buddhist, etc. But the word *dharma* does not have the same meaning as faith. The faith of an individual may change from Hindu to Buddhist to Christian to Moslem, etc. People have the ability to accept one faith and reject another, but *dharma* cannot be changed. It is the nature of every individual to render service, either to himself, his family, his community, nation or to humanity at large. This rendering of service cannot in any way be divorced from the living entity, and it is this that constitutes the *dharma* of every living being. Without rendering service, one cannot exist. The world goes on because we are all rendering and exchanging service. We must forget whether we are Christian, Moslem or Hindu, and we must understand that we are living entities whose constitutional position is to render service to the supreme living entity. When we reach that stage of understanding, we are liberated.

Liberation is freedom from temporary designations which we have acquired from association with material nature. Liberation is nothing more than this. Because we have material bodies, we take on so many designations; thus we call ourselves a man, a parent, an American, a Christian, Hindu, etc. These designations should be abandoned if we at all want to become free. Under no circumstances are we master. We are at the present serving, but we are serving with designations. We're the servants of a wife, of a family, of a job, of our own senses, of our children, and if we have no children we become servants of our cats or dogs. In any case, we must have someone, something to serve. If we have no wife or child, we have to catch some dog or other lower animal in order to serve it. That is our nature. We are compelled to do it. When we at last become free from these designations and begin to render transcendental loving service to the Lord, we attain our perfectional state. We then become established in our true *dharma.*

Thus Śrī Kṛṣṇa says that He appears whenever there is a discrepancy in the *dharma* of the living entities, that is to say whenever the living entities cease rendering service to the Supreme. In other words, when the living entity is too busily engaged serving his senses, and there is an over-indulgence in sense gratification, the Lord comes. In India, for instance, when people were over-indulging in animal slaughter, Lord Buddha came to establish *ahiṁsā,* nonviolence to all living entities. Similarly, in the above-quoted verse, Śrī Kṛṣṇa says that He comes in order to protect the *sādhus (paritrāṇāya sādhūnām). Sādhus* are typified by their toleration of all other living entities. Despite all inconveniences and dangers, they try to give real knowledge to the people in general. A *sādhu* is not the friend of a particular society, community or country but is a friend of all—not only of human beings, but of animals and lower forms of life. In short, the *sādhu* is an enemy of no one and a friend to all. Consequently he is always peaceful. Such persons who have sacrificed everything for the Lord are very, very dear to the Lord. Although the *sādhus* do not mind if they are insulted, Kṛṣṇa does not tolerate any insult to them. As stated in the Ninth Chapter of *Bhagavad-gītā,* Kṛṣṇa is alike to all, but He is especially inclined to His devotees:

samo 'haṁ sarva-bhūteṣu
na me dveṣyo 'sti na priyaḥ
ye bhajanti tu māṁ bhaktyā
mayi te teṣu cāpy aham

"I envy no one, nor am I partial to anyone. I am equal to all. But whoever renders service unto Me in devotion is a friend, is in Me, and I am also a friend to him." (Bg. 9.29)

Although Kṛṣṇa is neutral to all, for one who is constantly engaged in Kṛṣṇa consciousness, who is spreading the message of *Bhagavad-gītā,* He gives special protection. It is Śrī Kṛṣṇa's promise that His devotee shall never perish: *kaunteya pratijānīhi na me bhaktaḥ praṇaśyati* (Bg. 9.31).

Not only does Kṛṣṇa come to protect and save His devotees, but also to destroy the wicked *(vināśāya ca duṣkṛtām).* Kṛṣṇa wanted to establish Arjuna and the five Pāṇḍavas, who were the most pious *kṣatriyas* and devotees, as rulers of the world, and He also wanted to vanquish the atheistic party of Duryodhana. And as mentioned before, a third reason for His coming is to establish real religion *(dharma-saṁsthāpanārthāya).* Thus Śrī Kṛṣṇa's purpose for coming is threefold: He protects His devotees, vanquishes the demonic, and establishes the real religion of the living entity. He comes not only once, but many, many times *(sambhavāmi yuge yuge)* because this material world is such that in the course of time, after an adjustment is made, it will again deteriorate.

The world is so conceived that even if we make a very good arrangement, it will gradually deteriorate. After World War I an armistice was signed, and there was a short period of peace, but World War II soon came, and now that that is over they are making preparations for World War III. This is the function of time *(kāla)* in the material world. We build up a very nice house, and after fifty years it deteriorates, and after one hundred years it deteriorates even more. Similarly, when the body is young, people care for it, always lavishing affection upon it and kissing it, but when it grows old no one cares for it. This is the nature of the material world—even if a very good adjustment is made, it will in course of time be vanquished. Therefore adjustments are periodically required, and from age to age the Supreme Lord or His representative come to make adjustments in the direction of civilization. Thus Śrī Kṛṣṇa descends many times to establish or rejuvenate many different religions.

7

Knowledge as Faith in Guru and Surrender to Kṛṣṇa

In the Fourth Chapter of *Bhagavad-gītā* Śrī Kṛṣṇa concludes that of all sacrifices, the best is the acquisition of knowledge.

śreyān dravyamayād yajñāj
jñāna-yajñaḥ parantapa
sarvaṁ karmākhilaṁ pārtha
jñāne parisamāpyate

"O chastiser of the enemy, the sacrifice of knowledge is greater than the sacrifice of material possessions. O son of Pṛthā, after all, the sacrifice of work culminates in transcendental knowledge." (Bg. 4.33)

Knowledge is the best sacrifice because this conditional life is due to ignorance. The purpose of sacrifice, penance, *yoga* and philosophical discussion is to acquire knowledge. There are three stages of transcendental knowledge by which one realizes the impersonal aspect of God (Brahman realization), the localized aspect of God within the heart and within every atom (Paramātmā or Supersoul realization) and the realization of the Supreme Personality of Godhead (Bhagavān realization). But the very first step in acquiring knowledge is coming to understand that "I am not this body. I am spirit soul, and my aim of life is to get out of this material entanglement." The point is that whatever sacrifice we make is intended to enable us to come to the point of real knowledge. The highest perfection of knowledge is given in *Bhagavad-gītā* as surrender to Kṛṣṇa *(bahūnāṁ janmanām ante jñānavān māṁ prapadyate)* (Bg. 7.19). The *jñānavān,* not the fool, surrenders unto Kṛṣṇa, and that is the highest stage of knowledge. Similarly, at the end of *Bhagavad-gītā* Śrī Kṛṣṇa advises Arjuna:

sarva-dharmān parityajya
mām ekaṁ śaraṇaṁ vraja
ahaṁ tvāṁ sarva-pāpebhyo
mokṣayiṣyāmi mā śucaḥ

"Abandon all varieties of religion and just surrender unto Me. I shall deliver you from all sinful reaction. Do not fear." (Bg. 18.66)

This is the most confidential part of knowledge. From all points of view, if we make an analytical study of the Vedic literatures, we will find that the ultimate summit of knowledge is to surrender unto Kṛṣṇa. And what type of surrender is recommended? Surrender in full knowledge—when one comes to the perfectional point he must understand that Vāsudeva, Kṛṣṇa, is everything. This is also confirmed in *Brahma-saṁhitā:*

īśvaraḥ paramaḥ kṛṣṇaḥ
sac-cid-ānanda-vigrahaḥ
anādir ādir govindaḥ
sarva-kāraṇa-kāraṇam

"Kṛṣṇa, who is known as Govinda, is the Supreme Godhead. He has an eternal, blissful, spiritual body. He is the origin of all. He has no other origin, and He is the prime cause of all causes." *(Brahma-saṁhitā, 5.1)*

The words *sarva-kāraṇa* indicate that Kṛṣṇa is the cause of all causes. If we search to see who the father of our father is, and who his father is, and so on back, if it were somehow possible to trace our ancestry back through time, we would arrive at the Supreme Father, the Supreme Personality of Godhead.

Of course everyone wants to see God immediately, but we can see God when we are qualified and in perfect knowledge. We can see God eye to eye, just as we are seeing one another, but qualification is required, and that qualification is Kṛṣṇa consciousness. Kṛṣṇa consciousness begins with *śravaṇam*, hearing about Kṛṣṇa through *Bhagavad-gītā* and other Vedic literatures, and *kīrtanam*, repeating what we've heard and glorifying Kṛṣṇa by chanting His names. By chanting and hearing of Kṛṣṇa we can actually associate with Him, for He is absolute and nondifferent from His names, qualities, forms and pastimes. As we associate with Kṛṣṇa, He helps us to understand Him and dispels the darkness of ignorance with the light of knowledge. Kṛṣṇa is sitting within our hearts acting as *guru*. When we begin hearing topics about Him, the dust which has accumulated on our minds due to so many years of material contamination becomes gradually cleaned. Kṛṣṇa is a friend to everyone, but He is a special friend to His devotees. As soon as we become a little inclined toward Him, He begins to give favorable instructions from within our hearts so that we can gradually make progress. Kṛṣṇa is the first spiritual master, and when we become more interested in Him, we have to go to a *sādhu* or holy man who serves as spiritual master from without. This is enjoined by Śrī Kṛṣṇa Himself in the following verse:

tad viddhi praṇipātena
paripraśnena sevayā
upadekṣyanti te jñānaṁ
jñāninas tattva-darśinaḥ

"Just try to learn the truth by approaching a spiritual master. Inquire from him submissively and render service unto him. The self-realized soul can impart knowledge unto you because he has seen the truth." (Bg. 4.34)

It is necessary to select a person to whom we can surrender ourselves. Of course no one likes to surrender to anyone. We are puffed up with whatever knowledge we have, and our attitude is, "Oh, who can give *me* knowledge?" Some people say that for spiritual realization there is no need for a spiritual master, but so far as Vedic literature is concerned, and as far as *Bhagavad-gītā, Śrīmad-Bhāgavatam* and the *Upaniṣads* are concerned, there is need of a spiritual master. Even in the material world if one wants to learn to be a musician, he has to search out a musician to teach him, or if one wants to be an engineer, he has to go to a technological college and learn from those who know the technology. Nor can anyone become a doctor by simply purchasing a book from the market and reading it at home. One has to be admitted to a medical college and undergo training under licensed doctors. It is not possible to learn any major subject simply by purchasing books and reading them at home. Someone is needed to show us how to apply that knowledge which is found in the books. As far as the science of God is concerned, Śrī Kṛṣṇa, the Supreme Personality of Godhead Himself, advises us to go to a person to whom we can surrender. This means that we have to check to see if a person is capable of giving instructions in *Bhagavad-gītā* and other literatures of God realization. It is not that we are to search out a spiritual master whimsically. We should be very serious to find a person who is actually in knowledge of the subject.

In the beginning of *Bhagavad-gītā* Arjuna was talking to Kṛṣṇa just like a friend, and Kṛṣṇa was questioning how he, as a military man, could give up fighting. But when Arjuna saw that friendly talks would not make a solution to his problems, he surrendered unto Kṛṣṇa, saying, *śiṣyaste 'haṁ śādhi māṁ tvāṁ prapannam:* "Now I am Your disciple and a soul surrendered unto You. Please instruct me." (Bg. 2.7) This is the process. It is not that we should blindly surrender, but we should be able to inquire with intelligence.

Without inquiry, we cannot make advancement. In school a student who makes inquiries from the teacher is usually an intelligent student. It is generally a sign of intelligence when a small child inquires from his father, "Oh, what is this? What is that?" We may have a very good spiritual master, but if we have no power to inquire, we cannot make progress. Nor should the inquiry be of the nature of a challenge. One should not think, "Now I will see what kind of spiritual master he is. I will challenge him." Our inquiries (*paripraśnena*) should be on the subject of service (*sevayā*). Without service, our inquiries will be futile, but even before making inquiries, we should have some qualification. If we go to a store to purchase some gold or jewelry and we know nothing about jewels or gold, we are likely to be cheated. If we go to a jeweler and say, "Can you give me a diamond?" he will understand that this is a fool. He could charge us any price for anything. That kind of searching will not do at all. We first have to become a little intelligent, for it is not possible to make spiritual progress otherwise.

The beginning injunction of the *Vedānta-sūtra* is: *athāto brahma-jijñāsā.* "Now is the time to inquire about Brahman." The word *atha* means that one who is intelligent, who has come to the point of realizing the basic frustrations of material life, is capable of making inquiry. In *Śrīmad-Bhāgavatam* it is stated that one should inquire from a spiritual master about subjects that are "beyond this darkness." This material world is by nature dark, and it is artificially lighted by fire. Our inquiries should be about the transcendental worlds which lie beyond this universe. If one is desirous to find out about these spiritual worlds, he should seek out a spiritual master; otherwise there is no point in searching. If I want to study *Bhagavad-gītā* or *Vedānta-sūtra* in order to make material improvement, it is not necessary to find a spiritual master. One should first want to inquire about Brahman and then search out a master who has perfect vision of the Absolute Truth *(jñāninas tattva-darśinaḥ).* Kṛṣṇa is the supreme *tattva,* Absolute Truth. In the Seventh Chapter of *Bhagavad-gītā* Śrī Kṛṣṇa states:

manuṣyāṇāṁ sahasreṣu
kaścid yatati siddhaye
yatatām api siddhānāṁ
kaścin māṁ vetti tattvataḥ

"Out of many thousands among men, one may endeavor for perfection, and of those who have achieved perfection, hardly one knows Me in truth." (Bg. 7.3)

Thus out of many perfected spiritualists, one man may know what Kṛṣṇa actually is. As this verse indicates, the subject matter of Kṛṣṇa is not so easy but is very difficult. Yet *Bhagavad-gītā* also indicates that it is easy.

bhaktyā mām abhijānāti
yāvān yaś cāsmi tattvataḥ
tato māṁ tattvato jñātvā
viśate tad-anantaram

"One can understand the Supreme Personality as He is only by devotional service. And when one is in full consciousness of the Supreme Lord by such devotion, he can enter into the kingdom of God." (Bg. 18.55)

If we accept the process of devotional service, we can understand Kṛṣṇa very easily. Through it we can understand the science of Kṛṣṇa perfectly and become eligible for entering into the spiritual kingdom. If, as *Bhagavad-gītā* says, after many births we have to eventually surrender to Kṛṣṇa, why not surrender to Him immediately? Why wait for many, many births? If surrender is the end of perfection, why not accept perfection immediately? Of course the answer is that people are generally doubtful.

Kṛṣṇa consciousness can be attained in one second, or it cannot be had even after a thousand births and deaths. If we choose, we can immediately become great souls by surrendering to Kṛṣṇa, but because we have doubts whether or not Kṛṣṇa is actually the Supreme we have to take time to dissipate these doubts through study of the scriptures. By studying *Bhagavad-gītā* under the guidance of a bona fide spiritual master, we can remove these doubts and make definite progress.

It is the fire of knowledge that burns all doubts and fruitive activities to ashes. Śrī Kṛṣṇa gives the following information of the results of inquiring of the truth from one who has actually seen the truth.

yaj jñātvā na punar moham
evaṁ yāsyasi pāṇḍāva
yena bhūtany aśeṣāṇi
drakṣyasy ātmany atho mayi

api ced asi pāpebhyaḥ
sarvebhyaḥ pāpa-kṛttamaḥ
sarvaṁ jñāna-plavenaiva
vṛjinaṁ santariṣyasi

yathaidhāṁsi samiddho 'gnir
bhasmasāt kurute 'rjuna
jñānāgniḥ sarva-karmāṇi
bhasmasāt kurute tathā

"And when you have thus learned the truth, you will know that all living beings are but parts of Me—and that they are in Me, and are Mine. Even if you are considered to be the most sinful of all sinners, when you are situated in the boat of transcendental knowledge, you will be able to cross over the ocean of miseries. As a blazing fire burns firewood to ashes, O Arjuna, so does the fire of knowledge burn to ashes all the reactions to material activities." (Bg. 4.35-37)

The fire of knowledge is ignited by the spiritual master, and when it is ablaze, all the reactions to our works are turned to ashes. The reactions to our work, or our *karma,* are the cause for our bondage. There are good works and bad works, and in this verse the word *sarva-karmāṇi* indicates both. For one who wants to be liberated from this material bondage, the reactions of both good works and bad works are detrimental. In this material world we are attached to performing good works if we are situated in the modes of goodness. If we are in the modes of passion and ignorance, however, we do bad work in passion and ignorance. But for those who are going to be Kṛṣṇa conscious, there is no need of good work or bad work. By good work we may get a good birth in an aristocratic or wealthy family, and by bad work we may take birth even in the animal kingdom or in degraded human families, but in any case birth means bondage, and one who is striving for Kṛṣṇa consciousness is striving for liberation from the bondage of transmigration. What is the advantage of being born in a wealthy or aristocratic family if one does not get rid of his material miseries? Whether we enjoy the reactions of good work or suffer the reactions of bad, we have to take on the material body and thereby undergo the material miseries.

By engaging in the transcendental service of Kṛṣṇa, we actually get out of the cycle of birth and death. But because the fire of knowledge is not burning in our minds, we accept material existence as happiness. A dog or hog cannot understand what kind of miserable life he is passing. He actually thinks that he is enjoying life, and this is called the covering or illusive influence of material energy. On the Bowery, there are so many drunkards lying in the street, and they're all thinking, "We are enjoying life." But those who are passing them by are thinking, "Oh how miserable they are." That is the way of the illusory energy. We may be in a miserable condition, but we accept it thinking that we are very happy. This is called ignorance. But when one is awakened to knowledge, he thinks, "Oh, I am not happy. I want freedom, but there is no freedom. I don't want to die, but there is death. I don't want to grow old, but there is old age. I don't want diseases, but there are diseases." These are the major problems of human existence, but we ignore them and concentrate on solving very minor problems. We consider economic development to be the most important thing, forgetting how long we shall live here in this material world. Economic development or no economic development, at the end of sixty or a hundred years our life will be finished. Even if we accumulate a million dollars, we must leave it all behind when we leave this body. We need to come to understand that in the material world whatever we are doing is being defeated by the influence of material nature.

We want freedom, and we want to travel all over the world and all over the universe. Indeed, that is our right as spirit soul. The spirit soul in *Bhagavad-gītā* is called *sarva-gataḥ*, which means that he has the ability to go wherever he likes. In the Siddhalokas there are perfected beings or *yogīs* who can travel wherever they want without the aid of airplanes or other mechanical contrivances. Once we are liberated from material conditioning, we can become very powerful. Actually we have no idea how powerful we are as spiritual sparks. Instead we are very much satisfied staying on this earth and sending up a few spaceships, thinking that we have become greatly advanced in material science. We spend millions and millions of dollars constructing spaceships without knowing that we have the ability to travel wherever we want free of charge.

The point is that we should cultivate our spiritual potencies by knowledge. The knowledge is already there; we simply have to accept it. In former ages people underwent so many penances and austerities to acquire knowledge, but in this age this process is not possible because our lives are very short and we are always disturbed. The process for this age is the process of Kṛṣṇa consciousness, the chanting of Hare Kṛṣṇa, which was inaugurated by Śrī Caitanya Mahāprabhu. If, by this process, we can kindle the fire of knowledge, all of the reactions of our activities will be reduced to ashes, and we will be purified.

na hi jñānena sadṛśaṁ
pavitram iha vidyate
tat svayaṁ yoga-saṁsiddhaḥ
kālenātmani vindati

"In this world, there is nothing so sublime and pure as transcendental knowledge. Such knowledge is the mature fruit of all mysticism. And one who has achieved this enjoys the self within himself in due course of time." (Bg. 4.38)

What is that sublime and pure knowledge? It is the knowledge that we are part and parcel of God and that we are to dovetail our consciousness with the Supreme Consciousness. This is the purest knowledge in the material world. Here everything is contaminated by the modes of material nature—goodness, passion and ignorance. Goodness is also a kind of contamination. In goodness one becomes aware of his position and transcendental subjects, etc, but his defect is in thinking, "Now I have understood everything. Now I am all right." He wants to stay here. In other words, the man in the mode of goodness becomes a first class prisoner and, becoming happy in the prison house, wants to stay there. And what to speak of those in the modes of passion and ignorance? The point is that we have to transcend even the quality of goodness. The transcendental position begins with the realization *ahaṁ brahmāsmi*—"I am not this matter, but spirit." But even this position is unsettled. More is required.

brahma-bhūtaḥ prasannātmā
na śocati na kāṅkṣati
samaḥ sarveṣu bhūteṣu
mad-bhaktiṁ labhate parām

"One who is thus transcendentally situated at once realizes the Supreme Brahman. He never laments or desires to have anything; he is equally disposed to every living entity. In that state he attains pure devotional service unto Me." (Bg. 18.54)

In the *brahma-bhūtaḥ* stage one no longer identifies with matter. The first symptom of one's having become established on the *brahma-bhūtaḥ* platform is that one becomes jolly *(prasannātmā).* On that platform, there is neither lamentation nor hankering. But even if we rise to this stage and do not take to the loving service of Kṛṣṇa, there is the possibility of falling down again into the material whirlpool. We may rise very high in the sky, but if we have no shelter there, if we do not land on some planet, we will again fall down. A simple understanding of the *brahma-bhūtaḥ* stage will not help us unless we take to the shelter of Kṛṣṇa's lotus feet. As soon as we engage ourselves in the service of Kṛṣṇa, there is no longer any chance of falling down again into the material world.

Our nature is such that we want some engagement. A child may commit mischief, but he cannot refrain from mischief unless he is given some engagement. When he is given some toys, his attention is diverted and his mischievous activities stop. We are like mischievous children, and therefore we must have spiritual engagement. Simply understanding that we are spirit soul will not help. Understanding that we are spirit, we have to sustain the spirit by spiritual engagement. It is not uncommon in India for a man to give up all material engagements, to leave his home and family and take the renounced order, *sannyāsa,* and after meditating for some while, begin doing philanthropic work by opening some hospitals or engaging in politics. The hospital-making business is being conducted by the government; it is the duty of a *sannyāsa* to make hospitals whereby people can actually get rid of their material bodies, not patch them up. But for want of knowing what real spiritual activity is, we take up material activities.

By becoming perfect in Kṛṣṇa consciousness, knowledge and wisdom are found in due course of time. There may be some discouragement at first, but the word *kālena,* meaning "in due course of time," indicates that if we simply persevere we will be successful. Faith is required, as stated in the next verse.

śraddhāvāl̐ labhate jñānaṁ
tat-paraḥ saṁyatendriyaḥ
jñānaṁ labdhvā parāṁ śāntim
acireṇādhigacchati

"A faithful man who is absorbed in transcendental knowledge and who subdues his senses quickly attains the supreme spiritual peace." (Bg. 4.39)

For those who are hesitant and have no faith, Kṛṣṇa consciousness is very difficult. Even in our daily affairs a certain amount of faith is required. When we buy a ticket, we have faith that the airline company will take us to our destination. Without faith we cannot even live in the material world, what to speak of making spiritual progress. Where are we to keep our faith? In the authority. We should not book our ticket with an unauthorized company. Faith must be in Kṛṣṇa, the speaker of *Bhagavad-*

gītā. How do we become faithful? Control of the senses (*saṁyatendriyaḥ*) is required. We are in the material world because we want to gratify our senses. If we have faith that a physician can cure us, and he tells us not to eat such and such, and we eat it anyway, what kind of faith do we have? If we have faith in our physician, we will follow his prescriptions for cure. The point is that we have to follow the instructions with faith. Then wisdom will come. When we attain to the stage of wisdom, the result is *parāṁ śāntim*—supreme peace. Kṛṣṇa indicates that when one controls the senses, faith comes in the near future (*acireṇa*). Having attained that stage of faith in Kṛṣṇa, one feels that he is the happiest man in the world. This is our position. We have to accept the formula and execute it with faith. This faith must be in the supreme authority, not in a third class man. We must search out a spiritual master in whom we can have faith. Kṛṣṇa is the most authorized personality, but anyone who is Kṛṣṇa conscious can be accepted because a person fully in Kṛṣṇa consciousness is the bona fide representative of Kṛṣṇa. Having tasted the words of Kṛṣṇa's representative, we will feel satisfied, just as we feel satisfied upon eating a full meal.

ajñaś cāśraddadhānaś ca
saṁśayātmā vinaśyati
nāyaṁ loko 'sti na paro
na sukhaṁ saṁśayātmanaḥ

"But ignorant and faithless persons who doubt the revealed scriptures do not attain God consciousness.

For the doubting soul there is happiness neither in this world nor in the next." (Bg. 4.40)

Those who are hesitant in taking this path of knowledge have no chance. Hesitation is due to ignorance *(ajñaś ca).* For one hesitant in taking to Kṛṣṇa consciousness, not even this material world will be happy, and what to speak of the next life. The material world is already miserable, but if one has no faith it will be more miserable. Thus for the faithless the situation is very precarious. We may put thousands of dollars in a bank because we have faith that that bank will not close down. If we have faith in banks and airlines, why not have faith in Śrī Kṛṣṇa who is acknowledged by so many Vedic literatures and by so many sages to be the supreme authority? Our position is to follow in the footsteps of great authorities like Śaṅkarācārya, Rāmānujācārya and Caitanya Mahāprabhu. If we keep our faith by executing our duties and following in their footsteps, success is guaranteed.

As stated before, we must search out one who has seen the Absolute Truth and surrender to him and serve him. When this is done, there is no doubt about one's spiritual salvation. Everyone is anxious to see God, but in our present stage of life we are conditioned and deluded. We have no idea of things as they really are. Although we are Brahman and by nature jolly, we have somehow fallen from our constitutional position. Our nature is *sac-cid-ānanda,* eternal, blissful and full of knowledge, yet this body is destined to die, and while it is existing it is full of ignorance and miseries. The senses are imperfect, and it is not possible to attain perfect knowledge through them. Therefore it is stated in *Bhagavad-gītā* that if we at all want to learn transcendental knowledge, we must approach one who has actually seen the Absolute Truth (*tad-viddhi praṇipātena*). Traditionally, *brāhmaṇas* are meant to be spiritual masters, but in this age of Kali, it is very difficult to find a qualified *brāhmaṇa.* Consequently it is very difficult to find a qualified spiritual master. Therefore Caitanya Mahāprabhu has recommended *kibāvipra, kibā nyāsī, śūdra kene naya/yei kṛṣṇa-tattva-vettā, sei 'guru' haya:* "Whether one be a *brāhmaṇa* or a *śūdra* or a *sannyāsī* or a householder, it doesn't matter. If he knows the science of Kṛṣṇa, he's a bona fide spiritual master."

Bhagavad-gītā is the science of Kṛṣṇa, and if we study it scrutinizingly with all of our argument, sense and philosophical knowledge, we will come to know that science. It is not that we are to submit ourselves blindly. The spiritual master may be self-realized and situated in the Absolute Truth, yet we have to question him in order to understand all spiritual points. If one is able to factually answer the questions about the science of Kṛṣṇa, he is the spiritual master, regardless of where he is born or what he is—whether he be a *brāhmaṇa* or *śūdra* or American, Indian or whatever. When we go to a doctor, we do not ask him whether he is a Hindu, Christian or *brāhmaṇa.* He has the qualification of a medical man, and we simply surrender, saying, "Doctor, treat me. I am suffering."

Kṛṣṇa is the ultimate goal of spiritual science. Of course when we speak of Kṛṣṇa we refer to God.

There are many names for God throughout the world and throughout the universe, but Kṛṣṇa is the supreme name according to Vedic knowledge. Therefore Lord Caitanya Mahāprabhu recommended the chanting of Hare Kṛṣṇa, Hare Kṛṣṇa, Kṛṣṇa Kṛṣṇa, Hare Hare/ Hare Rāma, Hare Rāma, Rāma Rāma, Hare Hare as the supreme means for realization in this age. Caitanya Mahāprabhu did not make any distinctions as to caste or social position. Indeed, most of His foremost disciples were considered to be fallen in society. Caitanya Mahāprabhu even appointed Haridāsa Ṭhākura, a Mohammedan, as *nāmācārya,* or preceptor of the holy names. Similarly, Rūpa and Sanātana Gosvāmīs, two of Lord Caitanya's principle disciples, were formerly known as Sākara Mallik and Dabir Khās, and they were employed by the Mohammedan government. In those days, the Hindus were so strict that if a *brāhmaṇa* accepted service from a non-Hindu, he was immediately ostracized from Hindu society. Despite this, Rūpa and Sanātana Gosvāmīs were made principle authorities in the science of Kṛṣṇa by Caitanya Mahāprabhu. So there is no bar against anyone; anyone can become a spiritual master provided he knows the science of Kṛṣṇa. This is the only qualification, and this science in essence is contained in *Bhagavad-gītā.* At the present moment, thousands of spiritual masters are needed to spread this great science throughout the world.

We should understand that when Kṛṣṇa is speaking to Arjuna in *Bhagavad-gītā*, He is speaking not simply to Arjuna alone but to the whole human race.

Śrī Kṛṣṇa Himself declares that simply by knowing the science of Kṛṣṇa, Arjuna would not be subject to illusion *(yaj jñātvā na punar moham).* If we have a very good ship, we can easily cross the Atlantic Ocean. At present we are in the midst of the ocean of ignorance, for this material world has been likened to a great ocean of nescience. Therefore Lord Caitanya Mahāprabhu prayed to Kṛṣṇa in this way:

ayi nandatanuja kiṅkaraṁ
patitaṁ māṁ viṣame bhavāmbudhau
kṛpayā tava pāda-paṅkaja-
sthita-dhūlīsadṛśaṁ vicintaya

"O son of Mahārāja Nanda, I am Your eternal servitor, and although I am so, somehow or other I have fallen into the ocean of birth and death. Please pick me up from this ocean of death and fix me as one of the atoms at Your lotus feet." (*Śikṣāṣṭakam,* 5)

If we have the boat of perfect knowledge, there is no fear, for we can cross the ocean very easily. Even if a person is most sinful, if he receives the boat of the science of Kṛṣṇa, he can cross the ocean very easily. As stated before (Bg. 4.36), it does not matter what we were in our past lives. Because we were in ignorance, we may have committed so many abominable actions. Indeed, no one can say that he is free from sinful activity. But according to *Bhagavad-gītā,* this does not matter. Just by knowing the science of Kṛṣṇa, one becomes free.

It is therefore absolutely necessary that we seek knowledge, and the perfection of knowledge is to understand Kṛṣṇa. Today there are so many theories, and everyone claims to know the best way to live; therefore so many "ism's" have evolved. Of these, communism has become very prominent in the world. But in *Śrīmad-Bhāgavatam* we find the seed for spiritual communism. There Nārada Muni explains that in this material universe—whether one be in a lower, middle or higher planetary system or even in outer space—all natural resources are manifested by the Supreme Lord. We must understand that whatever exists in this world was not produced by any human being, but everything was created by God. No sane man can deny this. *Śrī Īśopaniṣad* enjoins:

īśāvāsyam idaṁ sarvaṁ
yat kiñca jagatyāṁ jagat
tena tyaktena bhuñjīthā
mā gṛdhaḥ kasya svid dhanam

"Everything animate or inanimate that is within the universe is controlled and owned by the Lord. One must therefore accept only those things necessary for himself, which are set aside as his quota, and one must not accept other things, knowing well to whom they belong." (*Śrī Īśopaniṣad, Mantra* 1)

Consequently all living entities, beginning from Brahmā, the highest demigod, down to the lowest ant, have the right to use natural resources. Nārada Muni points out that we can use these resources as much as we require, but if we take more than required, we become thieves. Unfortunately everyone is trying to conquer and predominate. Countries race to the moon in order to put up their flags and claim that planet. When Europeans came to America, they put up their flag and claimed it for their nation. This flag planting and flag waving is all due to ignorance. We do not stop to think where we are putting our flag. It is not our property, but God's. Knowing this is knowledge, and thinking that it is my property is ignorance. We have the right to utilize but not to claim or hoard.

If we throw a bag of grain into the street, pigeons may come and eat four or five small grains and then go away. They will not take more than they can eat, and having eaten they go freely on their way. But if we were to put many bags of flour on the sidewalk and invite people to come and get them, one man would take ten or twenty bags and another would take fifteen or thirty bags and so on. But those who do not have the means to carry so much away will not be able to take more than a bag or two. Thus the distribution will be uneven. This is called advancement of civilization; we are even lacking in the knowledge which the pigeons, dogs and cats have. Everything belongs to the Supreme Lord, and we can accept whatever we need, but not more. That is knowledge. By the Lord's arrangement the world is so made that there is no scarcity of anything. Everything is sufficient, provided that we know how to distribute it. However, the deplorable condition today is that one is taking more than he needs while another is starving. Consequently the starving masses are revolting and asking, "Why should we starve?" But their methods are imperfect. The perfection of spiritual communism is found in the knowledge that everything belongs to God. By knowing the science of Kṛṣṇa, we can easily cross over the ignorance of false proprietorship.

We are actually suffering due to our ignorance. In the law court ignorance is no excuse. If we tell the judge that we are not aware of the law, we will be punished anyway. If one has illegally amassed so much wealth and yet claims ignorance of his transgression, he will be punished nonetheless. The whole world is lacking this knowledge, and therefore thousands of teachers of the science of Kṛṣṇa are needed. There is a great necessity for this knowledge now. We should not think that because Kṛṣṇa was born in India that the knowledge of *Bhagavad-gītā* is sectarian or that Kṛṣṇa is a sectarian God. Indeed, in the Fourteenth Chapter Śrī Kṛṣṇa proclaims Himself to be the father of all beings, as pointed out previously (Bg. 14.4).

As spirit souls we are part and parcel of the Supreme Spirit, but due to our desire to enjoy this material world, we have been put into material nature. Yet in whatever species of life we may be, Kṛṣṇa is the Father. Thus *Bhagavad-gītā* is not meant for any particular party or nation but for everyone all over the world—even for the animals. Now that the sons of the Supreme are committing theft due to ignorance, it is the duty of one who is conversant with *Bhagavad-gītā* to spread this supreme knowledge to all beings. In this way people may realize their true spiritual nature and their relationship to the supreme spiritual whole.

8

Action in Knowledge of Kṛṣṇa

na māṁ karmāṇi limpanti
na me karma-phale spṛhā
iti māṁ yo'bhijānāti
karmabhir na sa badhyate

"There is no work that affects Me; nor do I aspire for the fruits of action. One who understands this truth about Me also does not become entangled in the fruitive reactions of work."(Bg. 4.14)

The whole world is bound by *karma*. We all know of the existence of microbes or germs which exist by the million within the measurement of one millimeter. In the *Brahma-saṁhitā* it is stated that beginning with the microbe, which is called *indragopa*, up to Indra, the king of the heavenly planets, all are bound by *karma*, the reaction of work. We all have to suffer or enjoy the reactions of our work, be they good or bad. As long as we have to suffer or enjoy these reactions, we are bound to these material bodies.

By nature's arrangement the material body is given to the living entity for his suffering or enjoying. Different types of bodies are acquired for different purposes. The body of a tiger is made for killing and eating raw meat. Similarly, the hogs are made in such a way that they can eat stool. And as human beings our teeth are made for eating vegetables and fruits.

All of these bodies are made according to the work done in past lives by the living entity. Our next bodies are being prepared according to the work which we are now doing, but in the previously quoted verse Śrī Kṛṣṇa indicates that one who knows the transcendental nature of His activities becomes free from the reactions of activities. Our activities should be such that we will not again become entangled in this material world. This can be made possible if we become Kṛṣṇa conscious by studying Kṛṣṇa, learning of the transcendental nature of His activities, and understanding how He behaves in this material world and in the spiritual world.

When Kṛṣṇa comes on this earth, He is not like us; He is totally transcendental. We desire the fruits of our activities, but Kṛṣṇa does not desire any fruits, nor are there any reactions to His actions. Nor does He have any desire for fruitive activity *(na me karma-phale spṛhā).* When we enter into business, we hope for profit, and with that profit we hope to buy things that will make our life enjoyable. Whenever conditioned souls do something, there is desire for enjoyment behind it. But Kṛṣṇa has nothing to desire. He is the Supreme Personality of Godhead, and He is full with everything. When Kṛṣṇa came on this earth He had many girl friends and over 16,000 wives, and some people think that He was very sensual. But this was not the fact.

We must understand the meaning of relationships with Kṛṣṇa. In this material world we have many relationships as father, mother, wife or husband. Whatever relationship we find here is but a perverted reflection of the relationship we have with the Supreme Lord. Whatever we find in this material world is born of the Absolute Truth, but here it is pervertedly reflected in time. Whatever relationship we have with Kṛṣṇa goes on. If we have a relationship in friendship, that friendship is eternal and continues from life to life. In the material world, a friendship exists for a few years and then breaks; therefore it is called perverted, temporal, or unreal. If we make our friendship with Kṛṣṇa, it will never break. If we make our master Kṛṣṇa, we will never be cheated. If we love Kṛṣṇa as our son, He will never die. If we love Kṛṣṇa as our lover, He will be the best of all, and there will be no separation. Because Kṛṣṇa is the Supreme Lord, He is unlimited and has an unlimited number of devotees. Some are trying to love Him as lover or husband, and therefore Kṛṣṇa accepts this role. In whatever way we approach Kṛṣṇa, He will accept us, as He states in *Bhagavad-gītā.*

ye yathā māṁ prapadyante
tāṁs tathaiva bhajāmy aham
mama vartmānuvartante
manuṣyāḥ pārtha sarvaśaḥ

"All of them—as they surrender unto Me—I reward accordingly. Everyone follows My path in all respects, O son of Pṛthā." (Bg. 4.11)

The *gopīs* or cowherd girl friends of Kṛṣṇa underwent tremendous penances in their previous lives to attain Kṛṣṇa as their husband. Similarly, in *Śrīmad-Bhāgavatam,* Śukadeva Gosvāmī says that those boys who were playing with Kṛṣṇa had undergone great penances and austerities in their previous lives in order to acquire Kṛṣṇa as a playmate. Thus the playmates, associates and wives of Kṛṣṇa are not ordinary living entities. Because we have no idea of Kṛṣṇa consciousness, we take His activities as triflings, but actually they are sublime. All perfection of our desires is there; whatever desires we have constitutionally will be perfectly fulfilled when we are in Kṛṣṇa consciousness.

Kṛṣṇa did not need any friends to play with Him, nor did He desire a single wife. We take on a wife because we have some desire to fulfill, but Kṛṣṇa is complete in Himself *(pūrṇam).* A poor man may desire to have a thousand dollars in the bank, but a rich man who has millions has no such desire. If Kṛṣṇa is the Supreme Personality of Godhead, why should He have desires? Rather, He fulfills the desires of others. Man proposes and God disposes. If Kṛṣṇa had any desire, He would be imperfect, for He would be lacking something. Therefore He says that He has no desire to fulfill. As Yogeśvara, or as master of all *yogīs,* whatever He wills is immediately realized. There is no question of desire. He becomes a husband or lover or friend just to fulfill the desires of His devotees. If we accept Kṛṣṇa as friend, master, son or lover, we will never be frustrated. Every living entity has a specific relationship with Kṛṣṇa, but at present this relationship is covered. As we advance in Kṛṣṇa consciousness, it will be revealed.

Although the Supreme Lord is full and has nothing to do, He works in order to set an example. He is not bound to His activities in the material world, and one who knows this also becomes free from reactional activities.

evaṁ jñātvā kṛtaṁ karma
pūrvair api mumukṣubhiḥ
kuru karmaiva tasmāt tvaṁ
pūrvaiḥ pūrvataraṁ kṛtam

"All the liberated souls in ancient times acted with this understanding and so attained liberation. Therefore, as the ancients, you should perform your duty in this divine consciousness." (Bg. 4.15)

The process of Kṛṣṇa consciousness requires that we follow in the footsteps of the great *ācāryas* who have attained success in spiritual life. If one acts by following the examples set by great *ācāryas,* sages, devotees and enlightened kings who have performed *karma-yoga* in their lives, he shall also become free.

On the battlefield of Kurukṣetra, Arjuna was very much afraid of being entangled in his activities by engaging in warfare. Kṛṣṇa therefore assured him that if he fought for His sake there would be no possibility of entanglement.

kiṁ karma kim akarmeti
kavayo 'py atra mohitāḥ
tat te karma pravakṣyāmi
yaj jñātvā mokṣyase 'śubhāt

"Even the intelligent are bewildered in determining what is action and what is inaction. Now I shall explain to you what action is, knowing which you shall be liberated from all sins." (Bg. 4.16)

People are actually confused as to what is work *(karma)* and what is not work *(akarma)*. Kṛṣṇa here indicates that even great scholars *(kavayaḥ)* are bewildered about the nature of work. It is necessary to know which activities are genuine and which are not, which are bona fide and which are not, which are prohibited and which are not. If we understand the principle of work, we can become free from material bondage. It is therefore necessary to know how to conduct work so that when we leave the material body we will no longer be forced to take another but will be free to enter into the spiritual sky. The principle of proper work is clearly stated by Śrī Kṛṣṇa in the last verse of the Eleventh Chapter:

mat-karma-kṛn mat-paramo
mad-bhaktaḥ saṅga-varjitaḥ
nirvairaḥ sarva-bhūteṣu
yaḥ sa mām eti pāṇḍava

"My dear Arjuna, one who is engaged in My pure devotional service, free from the contamination of previous activities and from mental speculation, who is friendly to every living entity, certainly comes to Me." (Bg. 11.55)

This one verse is sufficient for understanding the essence of *Bhagavad-gītā*. One must be engaged in "My work." And what is this work? It is indicated in the last instruction in *Bhagavad-gītā* in which Kṛṣṇa tells Arjuna to surrender unto Him (Bg. 18.66).

By the example of Arjuna we are to learn that we should only perform work which is sanctioned by Kṛṣṇa. This is the mission of human life, but we do not know it. Because of our ignorance we engage in so much work which is connected with the bodily or material conception of life. Kṛṣṇa wanted Arjuna to fight, and although Arjuna did not want to fight, he fought because Kṛṣṇa desired it. We have to learn to follow this example.

Of course Kṛṣṇa was present to tell Arjuna what his work was, but what about us? Śrī Kṛṣṇa was personally directing Arjuna to act in such and such a way, but just because Kṛṣṇa is not personally present before us, we should not assume that there is no direction. Indeed, there is direction. In the last chapter of *Bhagavad-gītā* the proper work which we are to perform is given.

ya idaṁ paramaṁ guhyaṁ
mad-bhakteṣv abhidhāsyati
bhaktiṁ mayi parāṁ kṛtvā
mām evaiṣyaty asaṁṣayaḥ

na ca tasmān manuṣyeṣu
kaścin me priya-kṛttamaḥ
bhavitā na ca me tasmād
anyaḥ priyataro bhuvi

"For one who explains the supreme secret to the devotees, devotional service is guaranteed, and at the end he will come back to Me. There is no servant in this world more dear to Me than he, nor will there ever be one more dear." (Bg. 18.68-69)

It is therefore incumbent upon us to preach the method of *Bhagavad-gītā* and make people Kṛṣṇa conscious. People are actually suffering for want of

Kṛṣṇa consciousness. We should all engage in spreading the science of Kṛṣṇa for the benefit of the whole world. Lord Caitanya Mahāprabhu came with this mission of teaching Kṛṣṇa consciousness, and He said that regardless of one's position, if he teaches Kṛṣṇa consciousness he is to be considered a spiritual master. Both *Bhagavad-gītā* and *Śrīmad-Bhāgavatam* are filled with information on how to become Kṛṣṇa conscious. Lord Caitanya Mahāprabhu selected these two books and requested that people in all corners of the world spread this science of Kṛṣṇa in every town and village. Lord Caitanya Mahāprabhu was Kṛṣṇa Himself, and we should take this to be Kṛṣṇa's indication of our proper work. But we should be careful to present *Bhagavad-gītā* as it is, without personal interpretation or motivation. Some people present interpretations of *Bhagavad-gītā*, but we should present the words as they are spoken by Śrī Kṛṣṇa.

One who works for Kṛṣṇa may appear to be working like anyone else in the material world, but this is not the case. Arjuna may have fought just like an ordinary military man, but because he fought in Kṛṣṇa consciousness, he was free from the entanglement of his activities. In this way, his work, although appearing material, was not material at all. Any action sanctioned by Kṛṣṇa—regardless of what it may be—has no reaction. Fighting may not be a very nice thing, but sometimes, as in the case of the battle of Kurukṣetra, it is an absolute necessity. On the other hand, we may perform work which may be very altruistic or humanitarian in the opinion of the world and yet be bound to material activity. So it is not the action itself which is important but the consciousness in which the action is carried out.

karmaṇo hy api boddhavyaṁ
boddhavyaṁ ca vikarmaṇaḥ
akarmaṇaś ca boddhavyaṁ
gahanā karmaṇo gatiḥ

"The intricacies of action are very hard to understand. Therefore one should know properly what action is, what forbidden action is, and what inaction is." (Bg. 4.17)

The path of *karma* is very intricate; therefore we should understand the distinctions between *karma*, *akarma* and *vikarma*. If we simply engage in Kṛṣṇa consciousness, everything becomes clear. Otherwise we will have to make distinctions between what we should do and what we should not do in order not to become entangled. In the ordinary course of life we unknowingly break some law and have to suffer the consequences. Similarly, the laws of nature are very strict and stringent, and they accept no excuse. It is a law of nature that fire burns, and even if a child touches it, he will be burned despite his ignorance and innocence. Thus we have to choose our course of action very carefully lest the stringent laws of nature react to bind us to suffering. It is therefore necessary to understand what work to do and what work to avoid.

The word *karma* refers to prescribed duties. The word *vikarma* refers to activities which are against one's prescribed duties. And the word *akarma* refers to activities which have no reaction at all. In the execution of akarmic activities, there may appear to be some reactions, but in actuality there are not. When we work under the directions of Kṛṣṇa, this is actually the case—there are no reactions. If we take it upon ourselves to kill someone, we are subject to capital punishment by the state government. Our actions are then called *vikarma,* for they are against prescribed actions. If, however, the government drafts us into the army, and we engage in battle and kill someone, we do not suffer the reactions, and this is called *akarma.* In the one case we are acting according to our own whims, and in the other we are acting under the direction of the government. Similarly, when we act under the direction of Kṛṣṇa, our actions performed are called *akarma,* for that kind of activity has no reaction.

karmaṇy akarma yaḥ paśyed
akarmaṇi ca karma yaḥ
sa buddhimān manuṣyeṣu
sa yuktaḥ kṛtsna-karma-kṛt

"One who sees inaction in action, and action in inaction, is intelligent among men, and he is in the transcendental position, although engaged in all sorts of activities." (Bg. 4.18)

One who can actually see that despite activities there are no karmic reactions, who understands the nature of *akarma,* actually sees things as they are. The word *akarmaṇi* refers to one who is trying to avoid the reactions of *karma.* By dovetailing his activities in Kṛṣṇa consciousness, although one may perform all kinds of activities, he is free. On the battlefield of Kurukṣetra, Arjuna engaged in fighting, and those on the side of Duryodhana also engaged in fighting. We must understand how it is that Arjuna is free from reaction whereas Duryodhana is not. Externally we can see that both parties are engaged in fighting, but we should understand that Arjuna is not bound by reactions because he is fighting under the order of Kṛṣṇa. Thus when we see someone working in Kṛṣṇa consciousness, we should understand that his work does not carry any reaction. One who can see such work and understand it is to be considered very intelligent *(sa buddhimān).* The technique is not so much in seeing what a person is doing but in understanding why he is doing it.

Actually Arjuna was engaged in very unpleasant activity on the battlefield, but because he was in Kṛṣṇa consciousness, he suffered no reaction. We may be performing some action which we may consider to be very good work, but if we do not perform it in Kṛṣṇa consciousness we have to suffer the reactions. From the material point of view, Arjuna's initial decision not to fight was a good one, but from the spiritual point of view it was not. When we do pious work, we get certain results. We may take a birth in a very good family, in the family of a *brāhmaṇa* or a wealthy man, we may become very rich or very learned, or we may become very beautiful. On the other hand, if we do impious work, we may have to take birth in a low class family or animal family, or become illiterate or foolish, or very ugly. Although we engage in very pious work and take a good birth, we will still be subject to the stringent laws of action and reaction. Our principal aim should be to escape the laws of this material world. If we don't understand this, we will become attracted by aristocratic families, wealth, or a good education or a beautiful body. We should come to understand that despite having all these facilities for material life, we are not free from birth, old age, disease and death. To caution us of this, Śrī Kṛṣṇa warns in *Bhagavad-gītā:*

ābrahma-bhuvanāl lokāḥ
punar āvartino 'rjuna
mām upetya tu kaunteya
punar janma na vidyate

"From the highest planet in the material world down to the lowest, all are places of misery wherein repeated birth and death take place." (Bg. 8.16)

Even on Brahmaloka, the highest planet in the material universe, repetition of birth and death are also present. We have to go to Kṛṣṇa's planet in order to be free from this. It may be very nice to be a rich man or a beautiful man, but how long shall we remain such? That is not our permanent life. We may remain learned, rich and beautiful for fifty, sixty or at most a hundred years, but real life is not for fifty or a hundred years, nor a thousand years nor even a million years. We are eternal, and we have to attain our eternal life. That we have not attained it is our whole problem. That problem can be solved when we are Kṛṣṇa conscious.

If we leave this material body in Kṛṣṇa consciousness, we will no longer have to return to the material world. The point is to avoid this material existence altogether. It is not a question of improving our condition in the material world. In prison a man may want to improve his condition to become a first class prisoner, and the government may give him A-status, but no sane man will become satisfied by becoming an A-class prisoner. He should desire to get out of the prison altogether. In the material world some of us are A-class, B-class or C-class prisoners, but in any case we are all prisoners. Real knowledge does not consist in simply getting an MA or PhD but in understanding these basic problems of existence.

yasya sarve samārambhāḥ
kāma-saṅkalpa-varjitāḥ
jñānāgni-dagdha-karmāṇaṁ
tam āhuḥ paṇḍitaṁ budhāḥ

"One is understood to be in full knowledge whose every act is devoid of desire for sense gratification. He is said by sages to be a worker whose fruitive action is burned up by the fire of perfect knowledge." (Bg. 4.19)

The word *paṇḍitam* means learned, and *budhāḥ* means well-versed. In the Tenth Chapter we also find the word *budhāḥ* in the verse *budhā bhāvasamanvitāḥ* (Bg. 10.8). According to *Bhagavad-gītā*, one may not be a learned man just because he has received a lot of education from a university. *Bhagavad-*

gītā says that he is a learned man who can see everything on an equal level.

vidyā-vinaya-sampanne
brāhmaṇe gavi hastini
śuni caiva śvapāke ca
paṇḍitāḥ sama-darśinaḥ

"The humble sage, by virtue of true knowledge, sees with equal vision a learned and gentle *brāhmaṇa,* a cow, an elephant, a dog and a dog-eater (outcaste)." (Bg. 5.18)

In India, according to Vedic civilization, a *brāhmaṇa* who is learned is considered to be the topmost man in human society. The *paṇḍita,* who is learned and gentle, sees such a *brāhmaṇa* on the same level with a dog or an outcaste who eats dogs. In other words, he sees no distinctions between the highest and the lowest. Is this to say that being a learned *brāhmaṇa* is no better than being a dog? No, that is not so. But the *paṇḍita* sees them as the same because he does not see the skin but the spirit. One who has learned the art of seeing the same spirit soul within every living being is considered to be a *paṇḍita,* for in actuality every living being is a spiritual spark, part and parcel of the complete spirit whole. The spiritual spark is the same in all, but it is covered by different dresses. An honored man may come in a very shabby dress, but this does not mean that he should be dishonored. In *Bhagavad-gītā* these material bodies are likened unto dresses which are worn by the spirit soul.

vāsāṁsi jīrṇāni yathā vihāya
navāni gṛhṇāti naro parāṇi
tathā śarīrāṇi vihāya jīrṇāny
anyāni saṁyāti navāni dehī

"As a person puts on new garments, giving up old ones, similarly, the soul accepts new material bodies, giving up the old and useless ones." (Bg. 2.22)

Whenever we see any living entity we should think, "Here is a spirit soul." Anyone who can understand such a spiritual vision of life is *paṇḍita.* Cāṇakya Paṇḍit gives the standard for education or the qualification for a *paṇḍita* in this way: "The learned man sees all women, with the exception of his wife, as his mother; he sees all material possessions as garbage in the street, and he looks on the sufferings of others as he would look on them in himself." Lord Buddha taught that we should not even hurt animals by word or deed. This is the qualification for a *paṇḍita,* and this should be the standard of life. It is therefore to be understood that one is to be considered educated in accordance with his vision of life and his activity in accordance with that vision, not by his academic degrees. This is the understanding of the word *paṇḍita* from *Bhagavad-gītā.* Similarly, the word *budhāḥ* specifically refers to one who is well-versed in the study of scripture. The results of such realization and scriptural learning are thus described in *Bhagavad-gītā:*

ahaṁ sarvasya prabhavo
mattaḥ sarvaṁ pravartate

iti matvā bhajante māṁ
budhā bhāva samanvitāḥ

"I am the source of all spiritual and material worlds. Everything emanates from Me. The wise who know this perfectly engage in My devotional service and worship Me with all their hearts." (Bg. 10.8)

The well-versed person or *budhāḥ* is one who has understood that Kṛṣṇa is the origin of all emanations. Whatever we happen to see is but an emanation of Kṛṣṇa. For millions and millions of years sunshine has been emanating from the sun, and yet the sun is as it is. Similarly, all material and spiritual energies are coming from Kṛṣṇa. As a result of knowing this, one becomes a devotee of Kṛṣṇa.

Thus one who knows that he must work in Kṛṣṇa consciousness, who no longer desires to enjoy this material world, is actually learned. Everyone is working in the material world due to lust *(kāma)*, but the wise man is free from the dictations of this lust *(kāma-saṅkalpa-varjitāḥ)*. How is this possible? *Jñānāgni-dagdha-karmāṇam:* the fire of knowledge burns up all reactions of sinful activities. It is the most potent of purifiers. Our lives have meaning and direction only in so far as we strive to attain this transcendental knowledge of Kṛṣṇa consciousness, *rāja-vidyā,* which is the king of all knowledge.

GLOSSARY

Ahaṁ brahmāsmi—the transcendental realization of oneself to be spirit, not matter.

Ahiṁsā—nonviolence to all living entities.

Akarma—activities which have no pious or sinful reactions.

Anumāṇa—evidence by hearing.

Arca-vigraha—the appearance of the Supreme Lord in a Deity form engraved from wood, stone or other matter.

Anasūyu—nonenvious.

Avatāra—one who descends from the spiritual universe into the material universe through his own will.

Bhagavān—Kṛṣṇa, who possesses in full all opulences—knowledge, wealth, power, beauty, fame and renunciation.

Brahmacārīs—celibate students.

Dāna—charity.

Jīvas—individual souls.

Kāla—eternal time.

Karma—duties prescribed in the revealed scriptures.

Karmīs—fruitive laborers.

Kīrtana—constant chanting of the glories of the Lord.

Mahātmās—great souls.

Mūḍhas—foolish men who are lower than animals.
Mukti—liberation.

Parama—supreme.
Prakṛti—material nature.
Prasādam—food that has been offered to Kṛṣṇa.
Pratyakṣa—evidence by direct perception.

Rāja-vidyā—the king of knowledge.

Śabda—the method of taking truths from a higher authority.
Sādhu—holy man.
Śakti—energy.
Saṁsāra—the cycle of birth and death.

Tapasya—penance.

Vikarma—activities which are against one's prescribed duties.

Yajña—sacrifice.
Yogeśvara—Kṛṣṇa, the master of all *yogīs*.

INDEX

OTHER BOOKS
by His Divine Grace
A.C. Bhaktivedanta Swami Prabhupāda

Bhagavad-gītā As It Is
Śrīmad-Bhāgavatam, Cantos 1-3 (6 Vols.)
Teachings of Lord Caitanya
The Nectar of Devotion
Śrī Īśopaniṣad
Easy Journey to Other Planets
Kṛṣṇa Consciousness: The Topmost Yoga System
Kṛṣṇa, The Supreme Personality of Godhead (2 Vols.)
Transcendental Teachings of Prahlād Mahārāj
Transcendental Teachings of Caitanya Mahāprabhu
Kṛṣṇa the Reservoir of Pleasure
The Perfection of Yoga
Beyond Birth and Death
On the Way to Kṛṣṇa
Elevation to Kṛṣṇa Consciousness
Back to Godhead Magazine (Founder)

A complete catalogue is available upon request.